OUR WISCONSIN RIVER

BORDER TO BORDER

NELS AKERLUND   JOE GLICKMAN

Pamacheyon Publishing, Rockford, IL

The Photographer

Nels Akerlund's initial foray into photography was an inauspicious one. At the age of two he was visiting his uncle, who had recently returned from Vietnam. The curious youngster ransacked his camera bag and exposed all his film. A 1992 graduate of the Rochester Institute of Technology, Akerlund, 26, has photographed Presidents Ronald Reagan, George Bush, Bill Clinton, Nelson Mandela, and F.W. de Klerk. His work has appeared in two books on Rockford architect Jesse Barloga, and in ONE DAY U.S.A. His last book OUR ROCK RIVER was published in 1995. Akerlund's love of photography and the outdoors has taken him all over the world, including a month-long hitchhiking trip from Seattle to the Arctic Ocean in Alaska, to church missions in Mexico and Columbia, and to concentration camps in Poland and Germany. The youngest man to kayak the entire 2,500-mile Mississippi River, he also completed the 1,000-mile Chicago-to-New York paddle marathon, the world's longest. Currently, he is working on TO THE TOP, a photography book on the highest peaks in each of the 50 States.
He lives in Rockford, Illinois with his wife Andrea and dog Champ.

The Author

Joe Glickman, a graduate of the University of Pennsylvania, is a 37-year-old freelance writer. His text has appeared in the New York Times, The Daily News, Newsday, The Village Voice, Outside, Men's Journal, Inside Sports, Adventure Cyclist, Runner's World, US, EcoTraveler, The Paddler, Sea Kayaker, Women's Sports & Fitness, and Brooklyn Bridge. He co-wrote (with Allen Barra) THAT'S NOT THE WAY IT WAS, a book about myths in sports. He is currently writing a book about his 107-day, 3,600-mile solo kayak trip from Montana to New York. He lives in Brooklyn with his wife Beth and daughter Willa.

Our Wisconsin River - Border to Border
Copyright © 1997
Pamacheyon Publishing

Pamacheyon Publishing
1332 Post Avenue
Rockford, IL 61103

Design and composition:
Kurt Mazurek
ColinKurtis Advertising & Design

Illustration:
Karna Erickson

Printing:
hc Johnson Press

Binding:
Reindl Bindery

ISBN: 0-9655081-0-2

Endsheet: In the late 1800's it was necessary to disassemble a lumber raft to run the narrows of the Wisconsin Dells. (H.H. Bennett Studio Foundation)

Previous: A fisherman enjoys the last rays of daylight. (Nels Akerlund)

This Page: A weathered gear on the historic Portage Canal. The coming of the railroad near the turn of the century rendered the canal obsolete. (Nels Akerlund)

Top Right: Aerial view of the river's humble origin at Lac Vieux Desert at the Wisconsin/Michigan border 427 miles from the Mississippi. (Nels Akerlund)

Bottom Right: The Mississippi (foreground) shadows the Wisconsin (center) where they meet near Prairie du Chien. (Nels Akerlund)

CONTENTS

Illustration: Karna Erickson

Above: "Whitewater" Dan and "Musky" Matt kayaking the Upper Wisconsin. (Nels Akerlund)

"Rivers are America's first highways, they're still highways, and they're my highways." —*Verlan Kruger, 74, who has paddled more miles than any man alive.*

THE CHIPPEWA CALLED THE headwaters of the river, wees-konsan, "the place of the gathering of waters." To the Winnebago, the word Wees-koos-erah meant "river of the flowery banks," or "the river." The Menomonie called it Wisc-coh-seh, meaning "a good place for home." In 1778 British map maker Jonathan Carver, the first English-speaking person to describe the river, said Ouisconsin meant "the river of a thousand isles."

These characteristics are all evident in the Winnebago legend about the serpent who had his home in the northern forests near the Big Lake. Once he left for the sea his great body wore a groove through the forests which filled with water.

INTRODUCTION
Border to Border

Less mighty serpents fled in all directions, creating the beds of smaller rivers and streams which now flow to the Wisconsin. Where there were rocks in his path, he slithered over them. Now the water rushes over them, making the loud hissing noise he made. Where he met a massive block of rock near the Wisconsin Dells, he thrust his head into a crack and struggled through, leaving twisted formations. Below the Dells he decided to travel to the west, finally reaching the Mississippi River.

As a kid growing up in Rockford, Illinois, Nels Akerlund spent much of his summer at a cabin with his family in Eagle River on the Wisconsin, fishing with his father and grandpa. During high school he often grabbed his camera and drove north to explore parts of the river. When Akerlund went to the Rochester Institute of Technology to study photography, the scenic river of his youth became a pleasant memory.

In 1994, Nels and I were part of a contingent of 24 kayak racers from seven countries competing in the Finlandia Clean Water Challenge, a month-long stage race from Chicago to New York. Nels and I suffered side by side for many hours on the Great Lakes, Erie Canal, and Hudson.

Off the water, he told me about his solo kayak trip down the Mississippi, which he had completed the summer before, the youngest person to do so. I talked about the mighty Missouri, which I had traveled alone for 77 days to get to the race in Chicago. One day, we decided, we would paddle another great river together.

The year after the race, Nels and his father, Dan, spent two weeks paddling the Rock River, a tributary of the Mississippi that practically runs through their backyard. For the next eight months Nels combed the 310-mile river in his battered kayak, taking pictures with his large-format camera. The result was OUR ROCK RIVER, a book which sold well enough to convince him that even people who never left the banks shared his love of the water.

When he decided to photograph another river, the Wisconsin was the obvious choice. Last May, father, son, friend Matt Pontious, and a fourth paddler—me—took to the water, setting out from the headwaters of the Wisconsin at Lac Vieux Desert at the Wisconsin/Michigan border and heading south and then

west to the Mississippi at the Wisconsin/Iowa border. Fifteen days and 427 miles later, we made it. Afterwards, Nels returned to the river countless times, in all four seasons, paddling (with 50-plus pounds of camera equipment) and driving to his favorite sites to capture the character of this sublime river. The result is OUR WISCONSIN RIVER - BORDER TO BORDER.

In October, Nels and I stood on an unnamed island that splits the river near Rhinelander. The right fork flows quietly over well-worn rocks; the left drops precipitously through a narrow shoot known as Whirlpool Rapids.

Above: Some of the northwood's most scenic country is along the Wisconsin River near Eagle River. (Nels Akerlund)

Next: A midday storm rolls in over Lake DuBay north of Stevens Point. (Nels Akerlund)

Above: A kayak is the ideal craft to get to the best fishing holes on the upper sections of the Wisconsin, which is too shallow and rocky for powerboats. (Nels Akerlund)

Right: This is perhaps the most famous image by H.H. Bennett, the man who brought the Dells to the masses. In 1886, he awed the public with his stop-action photography. (H.H. Bennett Studio Foundation)

Nels was there again to photograph the surging whitewater that has swallowed many a logger. We sat for a while watching the river churn past huge boulders. Brilliant sunlight highlighted the vivid fall colors. Leaves rustling in the wind complimented the sound of rushing water. Two bald eagles soared overhead. We felt thrilled and privileged to be in such a perfect place, but Nels was unsettled. "I hope I can capture this," he said. "I want people to feel the beauty." After a long pause he said, "I want my photographs to influence them."

The latter, of course, is a tall order, brought on in part by the momentary intoxication of the scene. But while it may be impossible for a two-dimensional medium to convey the full complexity of a three-dimensional landscape, it is worth noting that rivers like the Wisconsin have the power to inspire, and, more importantly, it is this spirit in which Nels took these photographs.

"*U*nlike mountains which can be seen and sometimes understood in a single climb, the personality of the river sleeps beneath a mirror of water reflecting back more than it allows us to see in a glance."
—*from Lower Wisconsin River Images*

THE "RIVER PIGS," MEN WHO PILOTED timber down the river, had the most dangerous job in the lumber business. With the spring thaw they would shove the half-frozen logs stacked on the banks into the swollen, icy river, and, using long metal-tipped poles and spiked boots, herd these twisting torpedoes to the mills for $2.50 a day. The most skilled (or perhaps the craziest) were the "whitewater hogs" who rode the lurching logs through the rapids. Getting crushed or drowning during the spring drives was so common the mill owners lost track of the body count.

Above: Early snowmachine in Eagle River, the "Snowmobile Capitol of the World." (Eagle River Information Bureau)

Right: Rainbow Rapids flows around one of the river's most beautiful islands downstream from Rhinelander. (Nels Akerlund)

CHAPTER ONE

Previous: Sunset on Eagle Lake at Eagle River's Chain of Lakes. (Nels Akerlund)

Above: Fall colors at their peak downstream from Eagle River. (Nels Akerlund)

Left: The Wisconsin River flows from right to left through Watersmeet Lake, along Route 70 just outside of Eagle River. (Nels Akerlund)

This May, Dan Akerlund nearly joined their ranks. It was our third day on the Wisconsin and the river was raging from the heavy snowfall the previous winter. Rainbow Rapids, the first serious stretch of whitewater, had nearly swallowed Dan whole the day before. So when he rounded a bend below Rhinelander in his kayak and heard the roar of Whirlpool Rapids, his pulse quickened and his heart sank. The current sucked him into a chute of boiling water funneled between boulders, and a four-foot standing wave engulfed him like a sock in a washing machine. When he opened his eyes, he was thrashing in the Class IV rapids ahead of his capsized boat. Nels pulled him out of the frigid water, but not before Dan had composed a mental farewell note to his family. From that moment on, we referred to him as "Whitewater" Dan.

From the beginning, death and daring have been part of the river's history. The first caucasian to set foot in Wisconsin was most likely a French lieutenant, Etienne Brule. For years he canoed the waters of the northern-most Great Lakes, living and trading with friendly Chippewa and Huron Indians. In 1633, however, his adopted Huron clubbed him to death and ate him.

A year later, the carnivorous Hurons accompanied Jean Nicolet, the first white to see Lake Michigan, to the shores of Green Bay. Clad in a flowery silk Chinese robe and holding pistols aloft in each hand, Nicolet was

Previous: Even at low water, Whirlpool Rapids, Wisconsin's most feared, is formidable. (Nels Akerlund)

Above: The author contemplating life on the river below Whirlpool Rapids. Note the high-water marks on the rocks. (Nels Akerlund)

Next: Rhinelander Flowage at sunset. (Nels Akerlund)

trying to impress a people he had heard might be Oriental; more importantly, people who perhaps knew the route to Asia. He headed up the Fox River, but all evidence indicates he stopped short of the portage that would have brought him to the river linking the Great Lakes and Mississippi.

In 1659 Pierre Esprit Radisson and his brother-in-law, Medart Chouart Sieur de Groseilliers, made the mile-and-a-half portage from the Fox and became the first whites to see the Wisconsin. Eleven years later, Jesuit Father Claude Allouez made the portage and paddled on the broad river in search of converts. No one knows how many souls he saved, nor how far he ventured, but scholars believe he made modest progress on both counts.

But the explorer to receive the most accolades was Father Jacques Marquette, who along with fur trader Louis Joliet and five voyageurs made the first recorded trip down the river. They set out on May 17, 1673, from the Upper Great Lakes to find the Mississippi, claiming as much North American real estate for France as possible. By June 7, they arrived in two bark canoes at a Mascouten village on the upper Fox. Guided by two Miami Indians, they located "a portage of 2,700 paces," according to Marquette. The Miamis refused to

accompany them further, fearing contact with the fierce Sioux. The shaken Jesuit wrote: [we are] "alone in the unknown country, in the hands of Providence." Seven days later, they reached the Mississippi. It took Marquette a month on the massive river to realize he was not heading to the Pacific. Instead he had found the best trade route from the Great Lakes to the Gulf of Mexico.

It was 1673: The Wisconsin River had been discovered.

There is a nervous excitement about committing yourself to a great river. We started paddling on a cold, clear Sunday morning in May at the headwaters, Lac Vieux Desert, which in French means Lake of the Desert. A shallow lake with roughly 20 miles of shoreline, it is divided equally by the border of Michigan and Wisconsin. The river flows out of the lake's southwest end and in less than a quarter-mile passes inauspiciously through two corrugated metal drainage pipes large enough for a kayak to maneuver through.

The clear, pushy water, more a stream than a river, twists in a series of switchbacks through a flat landscape of pines, birch, and maples. "The river is so winding," said one fisherman, "it's like a hog's intestine." Sitting low in a kayak, the tall reeds that line the banks obscured the view and made me feel like a kid lost in a cornfield. The river is so narrow deer can jump across—and often do. The endless sharp turns and beaver dams, which we often had to drag our boats over or around, made progress slow; however, the scenery was so peaceful, and the bald eagles soaring overhead so inspiring, that we didn't mind. By six o'clock, we'd paddled 40 miles and arrived in Eagle River, exhausted, but content to be under way.

Eagle River is obviously named for the magnificent birds which inhabit the 657,000 acres of the Nicolet National Forest and prey on unsuspecting fish in the more than 1,200 lakes in the area. Like the eagle, the trappers of the 1800's thrived here. The Eagle River flows

Above: Oneida County Courthouse in Rhinelander is known for its Tiffany glass windows. The building, constructed around the turn of the century, is on the National Register of Historic Places. (Nels Akerlund)

Right: This sleigh on exhibit at the Rhinelander Logging Museum hauled timber from the forest to railroad depots or to the river to be floated to a mill. (Nels Akerlund)

Next: The beaver, once the most prized pelt on the river, is now a kayaker's menace. This dam near Rhinelander is over five-feet high. (Nels Akerlund)

from a chain of 28 lakes, the largest inland freshwater chain in the world, and is a tributary of the Wisconsin. This waterway made it possible for trappers (lured by the abundance of beaver and the high price of pelts) to transport their goods out of the dense forest and down the Wisconsin.

Lumbermen descended on Eagle River for the same reason. When the Milwaukee, Lake Shore & Western Railroad arrived in 1883, the trees fell so fast the mills stayed open 24-hours a day. Fifty-eight million feet of lumber was harvested in 1885-86. By 1900, the timber was tapped out. However, Eagle River survived, and even prospered by promoting itself as a scenic playground for outdoor enthusiasts. Today this tranquil town is known as the "Snowmobile Capital of the World."

On our second day we portaged our first dam outside of Eagle River. Soon after we entered a set of rapids. Huge boulders distracted us from the submerged rocks which threatened to eat our fiberglass boats. That night we camped on an exquisite island just below the roar of Rainbow Rapids. The rapids were wilder than any we had ever paddled; so wild, in fact, that Dan took the first of his two unplanned swims in the freezing water. The following morning we headed to Rhinelander, 20 miles away. The twisting river was so high we cut corners through the flooded trees. The highlight of the day, other than the cheeseburgers we inhaled at a marina, were the two bald eagles we spied less than 30 feet away.

Anderson Brown, the so-called "Father of Rhinelander," arrived in 1871 in a birch bark canoe searching for timber stands to log below Eagle River; New Yorker F.W. Rhinelander, the president of the railroad, who agreed to build a rail connection to the area in exchange for half of Brown's 1,500 acres, established this logging town in 1883, but it was E.S. (Gene) Shepard who put Rhinelander on the map.

A river man and raconteur, Shepard appeared out of the woods in 1896 proclaiming that he had discovered a prehistoric beast—the Hodag—a fierce creature over six feet long and 250 pounds with two horns and six spikes on its back. To capture the fire-snorting creature he blocked the entrance to its cave with rocks, chloroformed it with a sponge attached to a pole, bound it, and brought it back to Rhinelander.

Shepard exhibited it at county fairs in a dimly lit tent, controlling its movements with wires. He gave lectures about the grunting brute. "It will eat nothing but white bulldogs," he told the press with a straight face, "and then only on Sundays." Word of the wild discovery spread across the country. Only when scientists from the Smithsonian were sent to examine his "Bovinus Spiritualis" did Shepard come clean: the body had been shaped by a wood carver, the horns came from a bull, the spikes were bear's claws, and the black, hairy skin was ox hide. The hodag burnt in a fire a few years later, but the greatest hoax in Wisconsin's history became the defining symbol and mascot of this once-booming logging town.

Above: The "boat-train," owned and operated by W.H. Bradley, was made up of a steamer which pulled six barges consisting of three sleeping cars, a dining room, kitchen, and an observation car. The "train" often traveled up the Somo River for as long as a week. (Tomahawk Chamber of Commerce)

"There is something about running water that has an enduring magic for man."
—*August Derleth, The Wisconsin: River of a Thousand Isles*

IN THE 1870s, THE HEAVIEST LOGGING in the country took place along the upper Wisconsin, where approximately 5,000 loggers toiled. Living all winter in the northwoods, laboring from dawn to dusk six days a week, eating pork, beans, biscuits, molasses, and tea—with a bit of beef and codfish thrown in—it's no wonder that by the time the spring drives rolled around these salty lumber dogs were itching to let loose in the towns along the river. "Booze, bawds, and battle" was their trinity of entertainment, with balladry a not-so-distant fourth. Who can forget such classics as "Ye Noble Big Pine Tree" and "The Hemlock That Stood by the Brook"?

One of the most popular songs of the time was "Round River Drive," about the legendary lumberjack Paul Bunyan

Left: Over 100 acres of pine known as "The Hog's Back" was once the private playground of W.H. Bradley. In 1910 the city of Tomahawk purchased the land for $10,000 and renamed it Bradley Park. (Nels Akerlund)

Above: The banks of the Wisconsin are rich with nature's intricate designs. (Nels Akerlund)

Above: Flanked by guides, nattily-attired fishermen pose with muskies and walleyes near Tomahawk in 1935. The man standing third from the right is the great-grandfather of Nels Akerlund. (Dave and Elaine Akerlund)

Right: Sunset over Lake Mohawksin in Tomahawk is enjoyed by man and beast alike. (Nels Akerlund)

and his fightin' crew: Big Ole, Chris Crosshaul, Axel Axelson, Happy Olson, Hels Helsen, Shot Gunderson, and of course, his blue ox, Babe, who stood 47 axe handles high. After his work in Wisconsin was done, Bunyan walked to the Dakotas, his huge footprints forming the many lakes in northern Wisconsin. Or so the story goes.

Another mythical figure, Whiskey Jack, was the rafts-man's counterpart to Paul Bunyan. Over seven feet tall and as strong as Samson, he drubbed all other rowdy raft pilots, town bullies, and wild Indians along the Wisconsin. No man could out-drink him. When his raft ran aground, Whiskey Jack picked it up and carried it to deeper water. He was, however, not an erudite gent, and signed his paycheck with a "X". One day, the bookkeeper noticed he'd signed with two "X's" and asked why. He had just gotten married, he explained, and thought now that he was hitched he ought to change his name.

But the romantic tales of the timbermen was largely the stuff of fiction. It was a harsh, even brutal, life, and most lumberjacks lasted only a winter or two. Loggers lost their limbs at an alarming rate. At night temperatures often plummeted so low the cooks had to thaw out the pancake batter in the morning. And speaking at meals was prohibited—supposedly to save time, but also to discourage fighting and organizing labor unions.

When we arrived in Tomahawk, 100 miles into our trip, "Whitewater" Dan announced that he was heading home. He'd

injured his leg during his frantic swim at Whirlpool Rapids and wrenched his arm
when he was trapped under a downed tree at Rainbow Rapids; however, the real
casualty was his confidence. The thought of more whitewater unsettled him, and
the Wisconsin, which drops 435 feet from Lac Vieux Desert to Merrill, has plenty
of it, especially in May. We were all surprised; Dan is a nervy man. When Nels
kayaked the Mississippi in 1993, Dan joined him for a week and was willing to
paddle at night to beat the heat despite the menacing barges. Traveling the length
of the Rock River cemented his love for rivers and deepened his already intense
bond with Nels, who was willing, even eager, to share his adventures with his
father. After a hearty dinner and plenty of persuasion, Nels convinced him to con-
tinue. "You can't leave," he joked, "you're the only one amongst us who ever picks
up the check."

Tomahawk was settled by Germaine Bouchard who built a tavern on the
river and started a ferry service. It was a risky venture, considering that from 1858
to 1886 he and his family were the only residents in an area that was once a

Left: The world's largest sprinkler? No, these imposing 1,315-feet long wooden pipes funnel the river around Grandfather Falls from the intake house to the power-house. (Nels Akerlund)

Above: Completed in 1939, these twin redwood tubes haven't seen much auto traffic in nearly 60 years. (Wisconsin Public Service)

Next: The smooth, sculpted rock at Grandfather Falls, once a raftsman's nightmare, highlights the river's power. (Nels Akerlund)

preferred Indian hunting ground. But in 1886 the Tomahawk Land & Boom Co., owned by W.H. Bradley, founded a sawmill. Then the railroad came through and suddenly Bouchard had plenty of company. Bradley built Tomahawk's first hotel, general store and bank, began a newspaper, and watched as the people came pouring in. Less than 20 years later, however, the timber was decimated and the boom ended as quickly as it had begun.

Twelve miles below Tomahawk are Grandmother Bull Falls and Grandfather Bull Falls (two miles long with three sharp drops), once two of the most treacherous rapids on the upper river. (The term "bull" is anglicized from the French "bulles," which means rapids.) The largest log jam in Wisconsin history took place in the mid-1880s at Grandfather Falls, when 80 million feet of lumber came to a grinding halt. For miles, logs were stacked like straws as much as 20 feet high. To free such a jam loggers with hooked levers, or peavies, climbed over the mountainous piles to pry loose key logs. Not infrequently, the man who mobilized the impasse was crushed. In 1872 alone, 40 river rats died.

Today the Grandfather Falls Hydroelectric plant diverts the river around this once-raging rapids, leaving it as tame as an old man in a rocking chair. The river simply vanishes into two enormous wooden pipes which transport it 1,315 feet from the intake house to the turbine-generators before returning it to its normal course. Hundreds of plumes of water spray through leaks, as if the world's largest wine barrel had been shot full of holes.

Above: The three-arched bridge over the Prairie River in downtown Merrill is a quarter-mile from the Wisconsin. (Nels Akerlund)

Right: Just outside of Merrill at Grandfather Falls, the watery rock garden offers a picturesque contrast to the turbines and powerhouses. (Nels Akerlund)

Our portage around the spouting pipes was a half-mile long, the longest of five carries around the dams that interrupt the 25-miles of wide, slow river between Tomahawk and Merrill. Unloaded, our kayaks weighed 55 pounds. Add another 50 pounds of gear and, in Nels' case, 60 pounds of camera equipment, and we probably outweighed a French trapper with a canoe full of beaver pelts.

That night we camped in a city park in Merrill. As we wolfed our dinner, I was struck by the unique dynamic between father and son. On the river Nels did the guiding, instead of looking to his father for guidance. On dry ground, they reverted to their usual roles. And yet, unlike most fathers and sons, they joked and confided in each other like best friends. Climbing into his sleeping bag, Dan emitted the weary but satisfied groan of a man who had paddled too many miles, and been slapped by a river that we'd all sorely underestimated.

"On a river, tranquility and excitement alternate every half mile, every tight, cliff-bound curve, every quiet pool where white flowers float on the reflection of the sky."
—*Kathleen Dean Moore, Riverwalking, Reflections on Moving Water.*

THE ROARING FALLS WERE A MEETING place where the Chippewa traded with the voyageurs for goods such as metal kettles, which made heating the sap for maple syrup much easier than using birch bark boilers. The first white settlers called them Big Bull Falls, supposedly because they sounded like a bellowing bull. The Chippewa were gone by 1850, but Walter McIndoe, a lumberman of influence, suggested the name be changed to Wausau, their word for "far away place".

McIndoe may have named the place, but George Stevens, the father of Stevens Point, made it an important mill town. A St. Louis lumberman living in New York, Stevens heard about the fabulous stands of white pine up north and in 1837

Above: The Jolly Family posing in front of Big Bull Falls (now Wausau), in 1866. (Marathon County Historical Society)

Right: Timber, once the life-blood of the Wisconsin, is still an important industry on the river. (Nels Akerlund)

Next: Peering over Wausau, Rib Mountain is 1,939 feet, the third-highest peak in the state and tallest along the river. It is believed to be over a billion years old. (Nels Akerlund)

CHAPTER THREE

came to see for himself. "It is decidedly the best mill site I ever saw or heard of in the Union," he wrote to his partners in St. Louis. The river was joined by two significant tributaries, the Rib and Eau Claire Rivers, and the rapids and falls could be harnessed for power. In 1841, after two trying years, he completed a sawmill and dam. By 1850 there were 14 mills and 1,500 Wausauites.

But entrepreneurs like Stevens were after one thing: short-term profit. Due to intense logging in the upper valley, the Wisconsin was prone to flash floods. On September 29, 1881, heavy rains forced more than 500 men to try and secure the guard lock at the Wausau dam with rocks. At three a.m., 60 million feet of timber jammed against the dam's piers, piling logs 25 feet high. By noon, two feet of water rushed over the dam, wiping out the tracks of the Lake Shore Railroad and tossing trains around town like toys. Mills and houses were submerged; the stone dam swept away. One account said: "The roar of the rushing waters could be heard for miles and the sight of the hurling, tossing timbers crashing into the foam-crested waves was a spectacle never seen before, or hopefully, ever again."

Today, Wausau has approximately 50,000 inhabitants, making it the biggest small city on the river. While the lumber boom disappeared shortly after the turn of the century, Wausau is now known for its insurance industry and, oddly, as one of the world's leading producers of ginseng. It also is the home of a dam-released world-class whitewater kayaking course.

We left Wausau on a sunny Saturday morning and paddled into a headwind that made each stroke feel like pushing open a barn door. Crossing open water on Lake Wausau, the rhythmic rollers washed over our decks. We stopped for the night on an island on Lake Du Bay, complete with a perfect sand beach. After a shrieking-cold dip in the recently thawed lake, we scrambled into our sleeping bags. We finally fell asleep around 11—only to be awakened an hour later by flashes of light so bright I could read my watch. The rain dropped in sheets; the howling wind threatened to flatten our tent; the thunder was so loud it was like trying to sleep in a bowling alley. Only when the storm passed around 4:30 a.m. was sleep possible.

Early the next morning, when most sensible people were still in bed, Matt Pontious, our third paddler, landed a 12-pound catfish and woke us with tales of his fishing prowess. This was ironic, since by the time we hit the Mississippi "Musky" Matt had unintentionally snagged

Left: "Wausau Midget," Jerry Sullivan poses along the river in a publicity stunt for Mathie Bock Beer in 1891. (Marathon County Historical Society)

Right: Water rages through Wausau during the flood of 1912. Note the railroad car swept off the tracks. (Marathon County Historical Society)

Below: The man-made whitewater course in downtown Wausau hosts world class canoers and kayakers every summer. (Nels Akerlund)

enough lures in trees along the banks to decorate a dozen Christmas trees. Later on, as we paddled south on the 1,125-acre flowage six miles above Stevens Point, the overcast sky grew dark and eerily still. The clouds turned grey and green and purple; the sky opened and hammered us with rain and hail. We might have passed the worst white water, but the river was reminding us not to lose our vigilance. As we neared Stevens Point, the wail of a siren pierced the thunder claps. At least two dozen power boats zoomed by, leaving us bouncing in their turbulent wakes.

As we hustled to shore, lightening struck the ground less than 50 feet away, sending sparks flying. A fisherman, who frantically motioned for us to jump into his truck, told us a tornado had touched down outside Wisconsin Rapids and was heading our way. We stowed our boats, and caught a ride to a hotel.

We were escorted into a convention room crowded with 500 dart players in town for a professional tournament. The majority appeared to be calming their nerves with spirits from the Stevens Point Brewery. All eyes turned to us—a drenched, dripping, foursome clutching kayak paddles. It was as if Jean Nicolet, resplendent in his Chinese robe, had stepped ashore to meet the Winnebagos. I felt like saying, "We are paddlers, take us to your leader!" Then a gregarious darter pointed to a cooler filled with "Point", chuckled, and asked, "Do any of you guys wanna play?"

Previous: The dam in Mosinee is one of 26 that harness the flow of the Wisconsin, earning it the reputation of the "hardest working river in America." (Nels Akerlund)

Left: The Dells of the Eau Claire, a one-and-a-half-mile-long gorge on the Eau Claire River, is a tributary of the Wisconsin. The river drops nearly 65 feet through the gorge forming walls 20 to 30 feet high. (Nels Akerlund)

Above: Established in 1857, Stevens Point Brewery is home to "Point" beer. (Nels Akerlund)

Right: With its 8,500 students, the University of Wisconsin at Stevens Point is known for its programs in business and paper science. (Nels Akerlund)

Below: A formally dressed fisherman displays the catch-of-the-day near Stevens Point. (State Historical Society of Wisconsin)

Next: Just north of Stevens Points along the shores of Lake DuBay stand symmetrical rows of Norway pines. (Nels Akerlund)

Left: Fall colors reflected on the backwater among the labyrinth of islands in the Wisconsin River Flowage outside Stevens Point. (Nels Akerlund)

Above: Pulled by ropes, the packed ferry at Wisconsin Rapids transported passengers, horses, buggies, and goods across the river. (State Historical Society of Wisconsin)

Next: Cranberry bog at Northland Cranberry, Inc. during fall harvest. The bogs are flooded with water diverted from the Wisconsin. The state is the largest inland cranberry-producing area in the world. (Nels Akerlund)

"Oh, what glorious Wisconsin wilderness! Everything new and pure in the very prime of the spring when Nature's pulses were beating highest and mysteriously keeping time with our own!" —*John Muir, The Story of My Boyhood and Youth*

IN 1831, DANIEL WHITNEY, WHO would become one of the richest men of his day, built the first sawmill on the Wisconsin not far from Wisconsin Rapids, ushering in an industry that would dominate the state for the next 75 years. Today, Wisconsin Rapids is home to Consolidated Papers, Inc., a sprawling plant with imposing smoke stacks that tower above the river like a battleship at port. But to us—paddlers consumed with mileage—Wisconsin Rapids (once known as Grand Rapids) had greater significance: it was halfway down the river, 216 miles from Lac Vieux Desert and 211 to the Mississippi.

Between "the Rapids" and "the Dells" stand Castle Rock and Petenwell lakes,

Previous: Sunset over Consolidated Papers Inc., Wisconsin Rapids. (Nels Akerlund)

Left: Aerial view of Petenwell (foreground) and Castle Rock Lakes, the largest reservoirs on the river. (Nels Akerlund)

Below: Ice fishing on Castle Rock Lake. (Nels Akerlund)

Right: High Rock, Wisconsin Dells. According to Indian legend, the striated sandstone formations were forged by a serpent slithering from Lac Vieux Desert to the Mississippi. (Nels Akerlund)

Wisconsin's largest reservoirs. We spent two days bashing into relentless wind on the shallow, seemingly endless waters. For the first time on the trip we wished we had motors instead of paddles.

When we finally entered the narrow channel of the upper Dells, we were surrounded by 100-foot high striated sandstone cliffs rising dramatically out of the deep, iced tea colored water. The Winnebago called the area Neehahkecoonahera—the place where the rocks strike together. The French explorers called it the dalles, or the narrow, rocky part of the river. In 1850, Byron Kilbourn, the railroad mogul who built the Kilbourn Dam that divides the upper and lower Dells, modestly named it Kilbourn City. In 1931, residents gave the area a more tourist-friendly moniker—the Wisconsin Dells.

By any name, it's worth a visit. Islands, gulches, canyons, and bluffs make up the state's greatest rock show, courtesy of the glacier that sculpted the Potsdam sandstone over the course of 30,000 years. In 1875, H.H Bennett, recently returned from photographing the Civil War, shouldered his cumbersome camera equipment to capture the essence of the Dells and bring them to the public's attention, much the way Ansel Adams would for Yosemite National Park.

Left: Looking upriver into the "narrows," where the Wisconsin is over 100-feet deep. (Nels Akerlund)

Above: Noah's Ark, America's largest waterpark, has the biggest wave pool in the Midwest. (Nels Akerlund)

Next: Romance Cliff, Wisconsin Dells. According to Indian legend, if a marrying couple tossed a burning ball of pine needles from the top and it went out before it hit the water, they would be destined for bad luck. (Nels Akerlund)

Paddling into caves and secluded caverns, we marveled at the dark moss blanketing the orange-tinted rock, streams pouring gently over a bluff into the river, the white birch growing out of dark cracks in the slick walls. While we oohed-and-aahed like kids in an amusement park, Nels had more practical concerns: "I don't know how I'm going to capture this on film," he kept repeating.

Actually, the best way to describe the twisted formations is simply to list the names of the figures and objects which draw countless camera-wielding tourists each year: The Jaws of the Dells, Chimney, Steamboat, Stand Rock, Black Hawk's Head, Devil's Bathtub, Pulpit Rock, Hawk's Bill, Hornet's Nest, Elephant's Back, Beehive, and the Grand Piano. Then there's the story that tells how when Paul Bunyan lay down to rest in the Dells, his head made the Sugar Bowl while his heels dug out caverns called, what else? Paul Bunyan's Heels.

While the terrain is stunning, the Dell's history is striking as well. In *River of a Thousand Isles*, August Derleth wrote how in 1869 Schuyler Gates, builder of the first bridge across the Wisconsin, was killed and robbed a half-mile from the Dells by Pat Wildrick, "a well-known desperado." Wildrick was plucked from the county jail at Portage and hanged from a tree—one of the few known lynchings in Wisconsin. There is the "legendary rock" from which Julia Le Morn jumped to her death due to unrequited love. There are scores of Indian mounds, including a bird memorial with a wing span of nearly 300 feet, and a water spirit mound 174 feet long. And there is the grave of the notorious rebel spy Marie Isabel High, a.k.a "Belle Boyd," who died of a heart attack in Kilbourn in 1900 during a lecture tour. The enigmatic inscription on her tomb reads: "Confederate Spy, Born in Virginia, Died in Wisconsin, Erected by a Friend." Not far away is the grave of a son of the famous abolitionist, John Brown.

The founding of the town of Kilbourn is also filled with melodrama. Five miles south stood Newport. In 1852, the town boasted 15 stores and three hotels

Above: A river pig running the rapids on a lumber raft near Kilbourn (now the Dells). (H.H. Bennett Studio Foundation)

Right: Pristine sand beaches make perfect camp sites. This one is in the Dells across from Black Hawk Island. (Nels Akerlund)

and was growing, largely because Byron Kilbourn, president of the Milwaukee and La Crosse Railroad and the mayor of Milwaukee, promised that a railroad would cross the river there. Four years later, he quietly purchased land north of Newport, secretly surveying the area at night by lantern. Within months of this being known, Newport became a ghost town. Later, it was learned that Kilbourn paid nearly a million dollars in bribes to acquire railroad grants. The scandal ruined him, but it wasn't long before the Dells became the state's most popular vacation-land—a curious combination of natural beauty and theme parks. The Indians have returned, but now they perform ancient tribal dances for the three million tourists who flock to the Dells each summer.

"That two such Rivers should take their rise so near each other, and after running such different courses, empty themselves into the sea at a distance so amazing… is an instance scarcely to be met in the extensive continent of North America." —*Jonathan Carver, from Travels Through the Interior Parts of North America in the Years 1766, 1767, and 1768.*

PIERRE PAQUETTE'S LAST WORDS before he was killed by a Winnebago Indian named Iron Walker were: "Shoot, and see a brave man die." Paquette, who was in charge of the trading post at Fort Winnebago in Portage for John Jacob Astor's American Fur Company, had been a legendary strongman: Weighing a rock-solid 240 pounds, it was rumored that his arms were so hard you could crack hickory nuts on them with a sledge hammer. Once, the half-French, half-Winnebago trader was hauling boats with a team of oxen across

Above: The steamer Wolf enters the Wisconsin River from the Portage Canal. (State Historical Society of Wisconsin)

Right: Surgeon's quarters in Portage, one of the remaining buildings of Fort Winnebago, overlooks the place where Marquette and Joliet crossed from the Fox to the Wisconsin in 1673. (Nels Akerlund)

Next: Winter falls on the Portage Canal, once a busy gateway from the Fox River to the Wisconsin. (Nels Akerlund)

CHAPTER FIVE
Portage to Prairie du Sac to Sauk City

the muddy portage between the Fox and Wisconsin Rivers. When one of his beasts could pull no more, he yoked himself in with his team and finished the job. Until his death in 1856, Paquette also owned and operated a ferry in Portage, the first on the Wisconsin.

The town of Portage grew up between the mile-and-a-half of land ...ating the Fox and the Wisconsin Rivers. The Fox runs into Lake Michigan; the Wisconsin joins the Mississippi. Linking Canada with the Gulf of Mexico, Portage was once the commercial crossroads of the Badger state. In 1850, 10,000 travellers made the land portage. In 1851, 13 years after construction began, the first steamers passed through the Portage Canal, although not without a glitch. The John Mitchell came from the Fox; the Enterprise from the Wisconsin. When they met in the middle, each captain refused to yield. The cranky, whistle-blowing captains attracted quite a crowd until they both withdrew. Only a few decades later, however, the railroad rendered the steam ship obsolete. Today the canal is a brackish monument to the past; the locks are rusted and the water still, but the limestone slab walls harken back to an engineering feat of major significance.

What hasn't changed, luckily, is the river below Portage. Except for the herds of buffalo, the river Father Marquette called the "Meskonsing"

Left: The south lock of the Portage Canal where it joins the Fox River. The Indian Agency House is in the background. (State Historical Society of Wisconsin)

Next: Commissioned in 1834, the canal was completed 42 years later after many delays. In 1854, Portage passed an ordinance forbidding nude bathing in the canal and Wisconsin River. (Nels Akerlund)

looks much as it did when he passed through in 1673: "It has a sandy bottom, which forms various shoals that render navigation very difficult. It is full of Islands covered with vines." This labyrinth of shifting sand islands forced us several times into water so shallow that we had to get out and pull. To stay in the "deep" water, we zig-zagged down the river like a dog sniffing for a bone. Historian Reuben Thaites, who canoed from Portage to the Mississippi in 1887, was only half-joking when he suggested the bottom be "lathed and plastered."

Still, as Thaites wrote, the landscape is "often of exceeding beauty." The Baraboo Range rises up at the river's sweeping bend to the southwest, creating 300 to 400-foot limestone bluffs covered with junipers, white pine, and cacti. This was our view when we camped for the night on one of the many flat sand-bars at the top of Lake Wisconsin. As the sun set, we sat by the fire watching three bald eagles soar over the lake in search of prey. Except for the occasional whack of a beaver's tale on the water, we luxuriated in the silence. That is, until we discovered we were in an exceptional echo chamber. Nels started Row, Row, Row Your Boat at the top of his lungs; Dan, Matt, and I chi until our maniacal laughter bounced off the valley's walls and drove all but the deafest beaver underwater.

Twenty-five miles down river from Portage are the "twin cities" Prairie du Sac and Sauk City, together known as Sauk Prairie or "Sac Prairie" in the many novels by resident August Derleth, Wisconsin's most prolific writer. Derleth, who hiked, paddled, and studied the river for most of his life, never left Sauk City because: "I am much attached to this corner of the earth, not only because it possesses great natural beauty, but because it affords me a necessary continuity."

Derleth's beloved hometown was once the domain of the Sauk Indians—300 warriors strong when English explorer Jonathan Carver came through in 1766. In his journal, Carver wrote: "This is the largest and best built town I ever saw....The streets are regular and spacious; so that it appears more like a civilized town than the abode of savages."

Left: Aerial view of dam north of Prairie du Sac. (Nels Akerlund)

Below: Diver at the Prairie du Sac dam preparing to descend into the frigid waters, April, 1912. (State Historical Society of Wisconsin)

Right: The Colsac II, the lone ferry still running on the Wisconsin. A ferry has crossed the river near Merrimac since 1835. (Nels Akerlund)

Next: Ferry Bluff, downriver from Sauk City and across from the Wisconsin's only nude beach, formerly known as "Bare-Skin" beach. (Nels Akerlund)

#73. DIVER (FRONT VIEW) AT WORK AT POWER DAM, PRA. DU SAC, WIS. PHOTO BY F. SEBERHART, APR. 19-12.

The most famous of the Sauks was Black Hawk, who was an infant when Carver visited. By 1831, Black Hawk was an intrepid Chief who rejected treaties with the U.S. government that he felt were designed to steal his sacred land. Pursued by 4,000 militia men, including 23-year-old Captain Abraham Lincoln, Black Hawk and his badly-outnumbered band of 500 warriors made it to what is now Sauk City. There, on July 21, 1832, the "Battle of Wisconsin Heights" was fought. Casualties were minimal —probably less than a dozen killed on both sides—before the Sauks slipped away into the night. But by July 29, Black Hawk's starving people, many of them old men, women, and children, were all but wiped out. Thus ended the sadly predictable Black Hawk War.

Eight years later, the most flamboyant pioneer of Sauk Prairie, Hungarian Count Agostin Haraszthy, "feasted" his eyes on the Wisconsin valley and began buying land. Historians claim he was not a member of the

Above: River men climbing out of their crude bunks on Cook Float around 1880. (H.H. Bennett Studio Foundation)

Right: Count Augustin Haraszthy planted the first vineyards in Wisconsin. His wine cellar is on the grounds of the Wollersheim Winery at Prairie du Sac. (Nels Akerlund)

Next: Gazing out over sprawling Lake Wisconsin near Merrimac. (Nels Akerlund)

Hungarian nobility, but when you wear a stovepipe hat, walk with a cane, go hunting in a green silk shirt and a wide crimson sash, and name a village after yourself, you can pass as a count pretty easily. (The town's name was changed from Haraszthy to Westfield, and then to Sauk City.)

Among his many enterprises, the bushy-bearded Count operated a ferry, opened a brickyard, grew the first hops in the state, raised pigs and sheep, and ran a steamboat from Sauk City to Prairie du Chien. One by one his schemes misfired. After 500 of his 2,000 sheep sizzled in a prairie grass blaze, he tried growing grapes, but was foiled by the harsh weather. In 1848, heavily in debt, the entrepreneur moved west and built a vineyard. Thus the self-proclaimed Hungarian Count who founded Sauk City became the father of the California wine industry.

Above: Owned by Daniel Whitney, one of the richest men of his day, this shot tower was built in 1831 on cliffs above the river across from Spring Green. It was used to manufacture lead. (State Historical Society of Wisconsin)

"**D**o not think that simplicity means something like the side of a barn, but rather something with graceful sense of beauty in its utility from which discord and all that is meaningless has been eliminated." —*Frank Lloyd Wright*

TURNER WILLIAMS, THE FIRST woman to settle in the Southern Sauk Prairie in 1843, suggested to railroad surveyors that the town be named Spring Green in honor of a nearby hollow that turned green each spring before the surrounding area. But the man who put the town on the map was its most famous—and flamboyant—resident, architect Frank Lloyd Wright.

Born in Richland Center in 1869, Wright inherited 200 acres from his grandfather in 1911 and built a house called Taliesin (Welsh for "Shining Brow") two miles south of Spring Green. An innovator who faced a barrage of criticism for his radical designs, Wright believed a building should emerge "organically" from its surroundings.

Of Taliesin, an earth-colored, sandstone structure nestled on a knoll, he wrote that he sought to build "a house a hill might marry and live happily with ever after." Despite the house's harmonious lines, it was doomed to tragedy.

Wright, who fathered six children with his first wife, had an affair with Mamah Cheney, the spouse of a client. Wright, Cheney, and her two children raised many an eyebrow when they moved into Taliesin together. In 1914, Wright was in Chicago on business when his chef locked Mamah and her kids in a room and set the famed house on fire; by the time the deranged man was caught he had also killed four workers who tried to escape, axing them to death. The press descended on the gory story like locusts and soon after Wright left for Japan.

Disaster visited Taliesin again in 1924 when lightening struck the house, causing $300,000 worth of damage. Incredibly, there was another fire in 1927. That same year the banks foreclosed on him. Wright wriggled out of debt and Taliesin eventually became a school for architectural students. Wright died in 1959 and was buried next to Mamah at the Unity Chapel near Taliesin. Despite his

Above: Frank Lloyd Wright, the Wisconsin valley's most famous citizen, wrote: "Early in life I had to choose between honest arrogance and hypocritical humility. I chose the former and have seen no reason to change." He died in 1959 at the age of 90. (State Historical Society of Wisconsin)

Right: Built by Wright in 1911, Taliesin was an architectural triumph but the site of a personal tragedy. (Nels Akerlund)

Next: Sunrise burning off the early morning fog near Spring Green. (Nels Akerlund)

request to rest in peace in the Wyoming Valley, in 1985 his third wife had his body exhumed and reburied next to her plot in Arizona. Even dead, Wright attracted controversy.

Perhaps there was something in the water in Spring Green that inspired architectural eccentricity. A few miles south of Taliesin, Alex Jordan, who owned his own construction company in Madison, started building "the house of his dreams" in 1946 on top of Deer Shelter Rock, a 60-foot chimney of stone. Part museum, part amusement park, part oriental temple, the 14-room House on the Rock confuses visitors while dazzling them at the same time: A 375-foot ramp ascends past tree tops to an entrance filled with bells, waterfalls, fireplaces and walls of rock—lots of rock. The house, which is the centerpiece of a sprawling complex on 40 acres, is home to the world's largest carousel, a four-story sea monster, and more guns, dolls, automated musical instruments, armor, and antique cars than any one man should have been able to collect in a lifetime. The best way to ponder Jordan's eclectic vision is to stare out of one of the 3,264 windows on the free-floating Infinity Room, which projects 218 feet over the valley like the elongated prow of a futuristic ship.

We visited both sites. Wright's graceful asceticism contrasted sharply with Jordan's fantastic shrine, and both seemed all the more dazzling after two weeks on the river. Back on the water, we turned our sights to the mosquitoes and sandbars between us and Lone Rock, 10 miles away. Curiously, the architectural marvels we'd visited stayed with us as we paddled through the valley, past rocky bluffs and the occasional fishermen. Both Wright and Jordan had loved the Wisconsin. They had roamed the banks we were sliding by, loved its moods, its solitude and beauty. We didn't discuss it, but we felt a little sad knowing we'd be off the river and back to our regular lives in less than two days.

Lone Rock, once nicknamed Devil's Elbow because the river takes a sharp turn to the north, is named after an imposing mushroom-shaped sandstone rock that became a landmark to the raftsmen because it was visible for miles. There is a story, perhaps more legend than fact, that a boat heading upstream from Fort Crawford with pay for soldiers at Fort Winnebago pulled next to the bluff across from Lone Rock to seek shelter from a storm. Just when they reached the far side, a rock slide buried the boat.

As August Derleth wrote, "If the story of the sunken treasure boat leans toward legend, that of Bogus Bluff leans toward history." Actually there are at least three different stories associated with the sandstone caves high above the Wisconsin River near Muscoda. The most preposterous was the discovery of bones of prehistoric animals and the skeletons of a vanished race in one of the caves. Another is about bandits who robbed a boat carrying soldiers' pay up to Fort Winnebago and were forced to leave the loot hidden on Bogus Bluff. The third, which has inspired many a treasure hunter to venture up the precipitous cliffs, involved some talented counterfeiters who in the 1870s holed up in the caves. Only experts could discern their ersatz currency from the real thing.

Nels decided to photograph Bogus Bluff. At the end of the day we shouldered his bulky camera gear, walked across Highway 60, climbed over a barbed wire fence, and trudged up the steep and crumbling incline in search of prehistoric bones, hidden treasure, or both. Soon we were panting like dogs. The mosquitoes were vicious and our legs felt useless. When Nels said, "Let's just go another 15 minutes," the three of us rejected that suggestion like a three-dollar bill. Bogus Bluff could keep its secrets for another day at least.

Left: Sandbars abound on the river from Lone Rock to Muscoda, often forcing us to get out of our kayaks to search for deeper water. (Nels Akerlund)

Above: Lone Rock was once a prominent landmark for raftsmen running timber downriver. (State Historical Society of Wisconsin)

Below: Once a Winnebago settlement, Muscoda, the Indian word for meadow or prairie, was a thriving town in 1879. (State Historical Society of Wisconsin)

"*T*he rivers run into the sea but the sea is never full, and the water returns again to the rivers, and flows again to the sea."
– *Ecclesiastes 1:7*

IN THE FIFTEEN DAYS SINCE WE PUT in at Lac Vieux Desert, we had watched the Wisconsin grow from a narrow, twisting stream to a surging, powerful, and capricious river. After 400 miles of paddling, the Mississippi, the great river the Winnebago called the "Father of Waters," was so close we could almost taste it. Boscobel, our last stop, was just 27 miles from the confluence.

Despite the Wisconsin's force and breadth, it remains an intimate river. The writings of early explorers and picturesque descriptions used by the Indians and voyageurs are, in many instances, still relevant today. The river is a connector of both time and place, which explains why we felt a kinship with many of the old-timers we met along the way. Many waxed poetically about the river, often using

Above: Boscobel's covered bridge, completed in 1874. (State Historical Society of Wisconsin)

Right: Dangling patches of ice after a winter thaw, Boscobel. (Nels Akerlund)

Next: Last light silhouettes the rolling hills surrounding Boscobel. (Nels Akerlund)

CHAPTER SEVEN

human terms. "We don't paddle like you guys," a woman from Eagle River said, "but we're always aware of her, like a farmer is the weather." A white-haired mechanic from Sauk City told us how as a child he had played on the shifting sandbars which sometimes disappeared overnight, "If she wants you, she'll take ya!"

As much as we'd come to love the river, after two weeks of hard paddling we were excited to reach Boscobel, our final stopover before heading home. The town's name means "beautiful woods" in French, but some say that the name came from a farmer who shouted for his cows Boss and Bell in the evening: "Come Boss! Come Bell!" In the 1850s, Boscobel was a busy agricultural center; today it's the kind of sleepy, tight-knit community that draws most of its 2,700 inhabitants to the high school football game. Any notoriety it enjoys these days is as the birthplace of the Gideon Bible.

On September 14, 1898, the Hotel Boscobel was so crowded that two traveling salesmen, both devout Christians, had to share Room 19. While rowdy men at the bar soothed their souls with spirits, John Nicholson and Samuel Hill stayed upstairs reading the Good Book aloud. The following year, the duo established the Gideon's Commercial Travelers' Association of America, and made it their goal to place a Bible in every room of every hotel in America. The Bible first appeared in a Montana hotel in 1908; since then, Gideon's (now based in Nashville) has distributed over 15 million Bibles worldwide.

Above Left: Built in 1863, the Boscobel Hotel is where two travelling salesmen, forced to share room 19, conceived the idea for the Gideon Bible in 1898. (Nels Akerlund)

Left: One of the highest spans on the lower Wisconsin, once the site of Jean Brunet's ferry, the bridge at Bridgeport is the last passenger crossing before the Mississippi. (Nels Akerlund)

Right: Villa Louis, the home of Hercules Dousman, Wisconsin's first millionaire, is located at the site of Fort Crawford in Prairie du Chien. (Nels Akerlund)

Above: The juncture of the Wisconsin (bottom) and Mississippi, four hundred and twenty-seven miles from Lac Vieux Desert, is where Pere Marquette wrote: "we safely entered the Mississippi with a Joy I cannot express". (Nels Akerlund)

Left: Built to run on water or ice, the "Lady Franklin", was used briefly as a ferry across the Mississippi in Prairie du Chien in 1859. (State Historical Society of Wisconsin)

When we stopped by the hotel around six o'clock on a Friday, the setting sun bathed the three-story stone structure in bright light. Just below the roof, "A. Bobel," the builder's name, was clearly visible. The hotel had been closed for years, but the homey bar downstairs was open. We asked the female bartender if we could see Room 19. She handed us the key and told us to go on up. We ascended the wide wooden steps to the darkened, run-down second floor. The room had a little plaque that read: "The Original Gideon Room." During John Kennedy's run for president in 1960 he and Jackie had stayed here. We stood in the empty room for a few minutes feeling a bit letdown by the hotel's shabby state.

At the bar we started talking with an artist, a history buff who told us about the arrowheads and pieces of pottery he'd found along the river. The artist was about to begin a huge painting on the Battle of Gettysburg, his most ambitious work. In 1861, he said, the Civil War volunteers gathered at the Boscobel railroad depot en route to Camp Randall in Madison, and in the town cemetery were buried 178 veterans. The Boscobel Hotel Preservation Committee, to which he belonged, was trying to raise money to restore the hotel. It was dark when we headed back to our tents on the river. It was good to know there were people trying to revive the hotel and that they still felt connected to Boscobel's past.

In the morning, our last on the river, it was raining and cold—only fitting since it had been 27 degrees when we started our journey at Lac Vieux Desert. Two hours after packing our soggy gear and starting out, the sun appeared. We passed under the Y-shaped concrete pillars of the bridge at, appropriately enough, Bridgeport, and in another six miles we were at the Mississippi. When Marquette reached this point in 1673

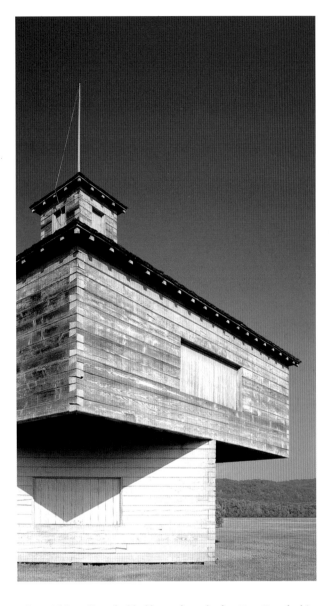

Above: This replica of a blockhouse from the first Fort Crawford is on the grounds of Villa Louis in Prairie du Chien. (Nels Akerlund)

Right: The view from a cave in Wyalusing State Park frames the meeting of the Wisconsin and Mississippi. (Nels Akerlund)

Next: Seen from Pike's Peak State Park in Iowa, the two rivers welcome more than 1,000 eagles who gather here every winter. (Nels Akerlund)

Endsheet: A Sunday afternoon cruise in the Wisconsin Dells around 1880. (H.H. Bennett Studio Foundation)

after so much toil and uncertainty, he wrote: "We safely entered the Mississippi on the 17th of June with a Joy that I cannot express." After following in his footsteps, it was easy to understand the intensity of his feelings.

And so with no fanfare except our own, our trip on the Wisconsin was finished. We paddled up the Mississippi to Prairie du Chien, roughly four miles above the confluence. Johnathan Carver, who visited in 1766, found a sophisticated community of about 300 Fox Indians. He called the area Dog Prairie after the Fox chief "Big Dog." The French later translated that to Prairie du Chien.

The first whites settled here in 1781, making it the second-oldest town in the state after Green Bay. Every May, the various Indians tribes of the Upper Mississippi country came with furs to trade. Because of its strategic and commercial significance, the Americans, British and French wrestled for control of the area, playing musical forts until the Americans established themselves permanently at Fort Crawford.

The dominant figure to emerge from the long and violent power struggle over the region was an ambitious trader for the American Fur Company named Hercules Dousman. Dousman, who arrived in 1826, worked for the unscrupulous tycoon John Jacob Astor. He foresaw the demise of the fur trade and purchased more and more land. By 1843 Hercules had become Wisconsin's first millionaire. Villa Louis, his stately manor, is located where old Fort Crawford once stood.

In River of a Thousand Isles, August Derleth, whose family lived along the river for four generations, wrote: "The river remembers past things, the aspects of life gone by forever..." He was referring to the Indians, the Jesuits, the voyageurs and traders, the raftsmen, and lumbermen who stripped the forests of their seemingly inexhaustible timber. Included were legendary figures like Black Hawk and his tragic war, lumber baron George Stevens, architectural giant Frank Lloyd Wright, wild dreamer Alex Jordan, and nature lover John Muir.

But I also like to think that Derleth, who referred to the Wisconsin as "a canoeist's stream," would have included a quartet of kayakers in that rich tapestry—four river rats who felt proud and privileged to have traveled all 427 of her miles.

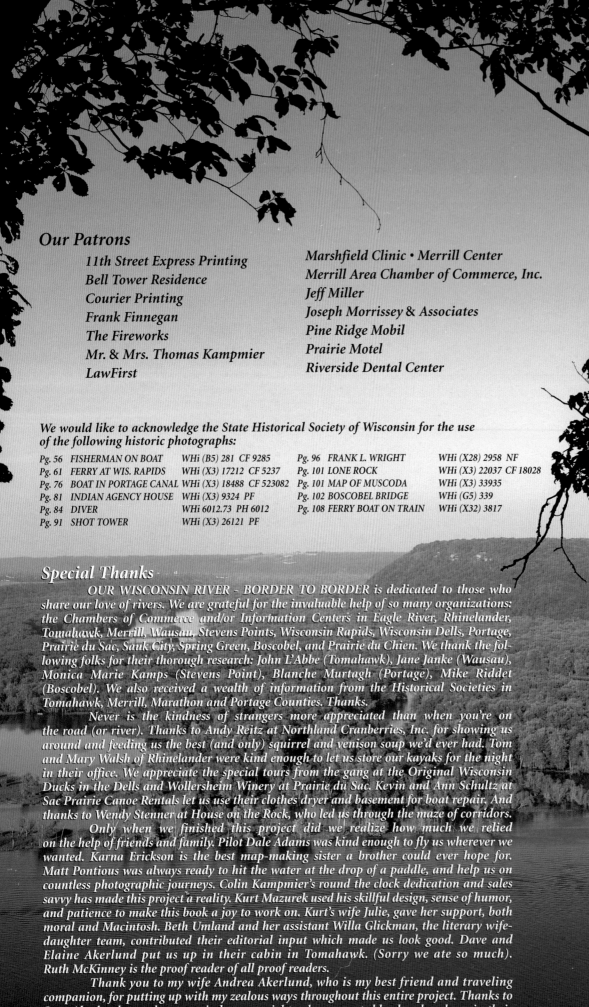

Our Patrons

11th Street Express Printing
Bell Tower Residence
Courier Printing
Frank Finnegan
The Fireworks
Mr. & Mrs. Thomas Kampmier
LawFirst

Marshfield Clinic • Merrill Center
Merrill Area Chamber of Commerce, Inc.
Jeff Miller
Joseph Morrissey & Associates
Pine Ridge Mobil
Prairie Motel
Riverside Dental Center

We would like to acknowledge the State Historical Society of Wisconsin for the use
of the following historic photographs:

Pg. 56	FISHERMAN ON BOAT	WHi (B5) 281 CF 9285	
Pg. 61	FERRY AT WIS. RAPIDS	WHi (X3) 17212 CF 5237	
Pg. 76	BOAT IN PORTAGE CANAL	WHi (X3) 18488 CF 523082	
Pg. 81	INDIAN AGENCY HOUSE	WHi (X3) 9324 PF	
Pg. 84	DIVER	WHi 6012.73 PH 6012	
Pg. 91	SHOT TOWER	WHi (X3) 26121 PF	

Pg. 96	FRANK L. WRIGHT	WHi (X28) 2958 NF
Pg. 101	LONE ROCK	WHi (X3) 22037 CF 18028
Pg. 101	MAP OF MUSCODA	WHi (X3) 33935
Pg. 102	BOSCOBEL BRIDGE	WHi (G5) 339
Pg. 108	FERRY BOAT ON TRAIN	WHi (X32) 3817

Special Thanks

OUR WISCONSIN RIVER - BORDER TO BORDER is dedicated to those who
share our love of rivers. We are grateful for the invaluable help of so many organizations:
the Chambers of Commerce and/or Information Centers in Eagle River, Rhinelander,
Tomahawk, Merrill, Wausau, Stevens Points, Wisconsin Rapids, Wisconsin Dells, Portage,
Prairie du Sac, Sauk City, Spring Green, Boscobel, and Prairie du Chien. We thank the fol-
lowing folks for their thorough research: John L'Abbe (Tomahawk), Jane Janke (Wausau),
Monica Marie Kamps (Stevens Point), Blanche Murtagh (Portage), Mike Riddet
(Boscobel). We also received a wealth of information from the Historical Societies in
Tomahawk, Merrill, Marathon and Portage Counties. Thanks.

Never is the kindness of strangers more appreciated than when you're on
the road (or river). Thanks to Andy Reitz at Northland Cranberries, Inc. for showing us
around and feeding us the best (and only) squirrel and venison soup we'd ever had. Tom
and Mary Walsh of Rhinelander were kind enough to let us store our kayaks for the night
in their office. We appreciate the special tours from the gang at the Original Wisconsin
Ducks in the Dells and Wollersheim Winery at Prairie du Sac. Kevin and Ann Schultz at
Sac Prairie Canoe Rentals let us use their clothes dryer and basement for boat repair. And
thanks to Wendy Stenner at House on the Rock, who led us through the maze of corridors.

Only when we finished this project did we realize how much we relied
on the help of friends and family. Pilot Dale Adams was kind enough to fly us wherever we
wanted. Karna Erickson is the best map-making sister a brother could ever hope for.
Matt Pontious was always ready to hit the water at the drop of a paddle, and help us on
countless photographic journeys. Colin Kampmier's round the clock dedication and sales
savvy has made this project a reality. Kurt Mazurek used his skillful design, sense of humor,
and patience to make this book a joy to work on. Kurt's wife Julie, gave her support, both
moral and Macintosh. Beth Umland and her assistant Willa Glickman, the literary wife-
daughter team, contributed their editorial input which made us look good. Dave and
Elaine Akerlund put us up in their cabin in Tomahawk. (Sorry we ate so much).
Ruth McKinney is the proof reader of all proof readers.

Thank you to my wife Andrea Akerlund, who is my best friend and traveling
companion, for putting up with my zealous ways throughout this entire project. Thanks to
Sara Akerlund, an adventurer in her own right, who supported husband and son in their
journey. And finally, thanks to "Whitewater" Dan Akerlund for being a great father and
friend to the three of us.

Spaghetti Art Ware

Poodles and
Other Collectible Ceramics

Wanda Gessner

4880 Lower Valley Rd. Atglen, PA 19310 USA

Dedication

To my husband, Robert, for all his help in typing, editing, and correcting my work. Also to my daughter, Robin, for giving up her free time to sort and label all photographs and negatives.

Designed by Bonnie M. Hensley
BernhardMod BT/Times New Roman

ISBN: 0-7643-0511-5
Printed in China
1 2 3 4

Published by Schiffer Publishing Ltd.
4880 Lower Valley Road Atglen, PA 19310
Phone: (610) 593-1777; Fax: (610) 593-2002
E-mail: Schifferbk@aol.com
Please write for a free catalog.
This book may be purchased from the publisher.
Please include $3.95 for shipping.

Try your bookstore first.
We are interested in hearing from authors
with book ideas on related subjects.

If you have an unusual piece and would like to share it, send a photo or write to Wanda Gessner care of the publisher.

This book is only to be used as a guide and is not intended to set market prices. Prices vary from dealer to dealer and collector to collector. The initial cost of a piece plays a large role in individual pricing, along with supply and demand. We assume no responsibility for any persons using prices herein or losses that may occur by doing so.

Contents

Introduction

In the following pages I have tried to capture the many faces of man's best friend. Who knows when the fascination for poodles began, but the breed has been portrayed in all shapes, sizes, and colors since the 1930s. These poodles were made to look intelligent, happy, sad, dumb, sophisticated, studious, and musical. Each and every poodle had his or her own personality. Their popularity reached a peak in the 1950s and almost every home had one. Most of these poodles, if not all, were made in Japan.

Though it leant itself perfectly to the portrayal of poodles, during the height of its popularity spaghetti art was also applied to a number of ceramic figurines. Christmas items were abundant and Santa Claus was very popular. Like the poodles, he was given many shapes and faces. Salt and pepper shakers were also very popular. Items such as planters, candle holders, piggy banks, and candy holders were also available. Other items that could be found were figures of children, animals, bells, night lights, ashtrays, cigarette holders, lamps, compotes, pincushions, and scissor holders.

This type of ceramic is very fragile and therefore hard to clean. Thus, as time went by the spaghetti strands became shorter and more massed and swirled. Then the amount of application began to decrease. Soon the spaghetti strands were replaced by small clumps of ceramics, thick at first and followed by more spacious, smoother applications. Thereafter this art form was phased out and an era was over.

The types of ceramic paints and glazes used during the spaghetti art era were not of the best quality. Many were simply painted after their first firing, and the paint was lost in subsequent washings. Therefore it's very difficult to find pieces that aren't peeling. This is obvious in the Christmas collection. Unfortunately the small pieces have not survived and the larger ones are very hard to find. Most pieces were stamped with ink or had stickers on their bottoms, but years of washing has removed most of the identifying marks. Since these figurines were imports, there may not be any reference material available.

Manufacturers and Importers

1. PC Lefton	Japan		22. ESD	Japan
2. Lefton China	Japan		23. Sonsco	Japan
3. Kreiss and Company	Japan		24. Inarco Ceramics	Japan
4. Napco Ceramics	Japan		25. California Creations by Bradley	Japan
5. Botiques by Essay	Japan		26. Relco Imports	Japan
6. Kelvin Exclusives	Japan		27. Original Arnart Creations	Japan
7. Fine Quality China Company	Japan		28. Lenwill China	Japan
8. Classica Inc.	Japan		29. Commodor	Japan
9. Walls	Japan		30. Zali Design Fine China	Japan
10. Rhoda Poodle	Japan		31. Robyn Patent	Japan
11. Thames Company	Japan		32. Royal China Company	Japan
12. Remco	Japan		33. Irving Rice and Company Inc.	Japan
13. Tilso	Japan		34. Lipper and Mann Creations	Japan
14. Enesco Imports	Japan		35. Samson Import Company	Japan
15. Reliable Glassware	Japan		36. Cornet	Japan
16. Holt Howard	Japan		37. Royal Sealy	Japan
17. Vcagco Ceramics	Japan		38. Nov Company	Japan
18. Rice and Company	Japan		39. Ries Company	Japan
19. Reubens	Japan		40. National Potteries Co.	Japan
20. Shafford	Japan		41. Artmark Originals	Japan
21. West Pac	Japan		42. Relpo Original Ceramics	Japan.

Grading Your Figurines

Mint Condition
No color fading, cracking, or peeling of paint. Piece is in like new. No spaghetti damage. Rhinestones intact and bright. All accessories.

Near Mint Condition
Very minor fading of paint. Rhinestones in intact and bright. No spaghetti damage. All accessories.

Good Condition
Minor wear and fading of colors. No peeling of paint. No rhinestones missing. Not all rhinestones are bright. No visible damage to spaghetti decorations. No chips or cracks. With some accessories.

Fair Condition
Figurine not chipped or broken. Most paint washed off or peeling. Some but no extreme damage to spaghetti decorations. Missing some rhinestones. No accessories.

Materials and Description

These poodles are made of ceramic material, porcelain, or red clay. The hair was applied three different ways, thus giving us three different textures. To achieve the hair-like strands, ceramic clay was forced through a tea strainer or facsimile then affixed to the body of the poodle. It was made to stick straight out for a long-haired look, pressed to give it a matted look, or layered and swirled on for a look of depth and a curly appearance. Some collectors and dealers call the resulting appearance "spaghetti" or "coleslaw."

The process creates a hair-like surface that is very fragile and hard to clean. Rhinestones were frequently combined with spaghetti art as eyes or on dog collars. Pearls were also used on collars and surfaces for decoration. Ceramic flowers were applied to hats and heads. Some netting was used, small neckless-type chains were also used to attach puppies to moms, and thin wires were used to hold up umbrellas.

Bottom Marks

Shafford

E.S.D.

West Pac

Thames Company

Original Arnart Creations

Ries Hand Decorated

G. Nov. Company

Japan

Royal Sealy

Irving W. Rice & Co.

Wales

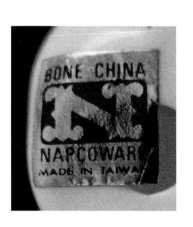

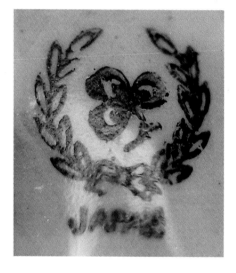

NapcoWare

Kelvin Exclusives

Japan

H.B.

Lefton Exclusives

Vcagco Ceramics

Zali Design   Japan   Japan

Kreiss & Company   Tilso

Lipper & Mann Creations   Relpo Original Ceramic   Royal

Inarco   Rubens   Napco

Samson Import Co.

Commodore

Boutiques by Essay

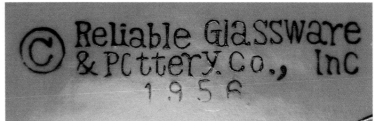

Reliable Glassware & Pottery Co., Inc.

Relpo

Lenville China, Ardolt Verithin

Lipper & Mann

Holt Howard

Lefton, 1957

California Creations by Bradley

Coronet

Japan

Holt Howard, 1958

Napco

Japan

Pacific Imports

Classica Inc.   Fine Quality Japan

National Potteries Co.   Relco   Japan

Enesco   Artmark Originals

Dogs

Both poodles are white and wear gold collars. Gold accents on sofa. Kelvin Exclusives. Made in Japan. 4.5" tall, 3.5" long. $28-40.

White poodle wears blue bonnet with multi-colored flowers and has a red bow on the back of her neck. Made in Japan. 4" tall, 5" long. $16-26.

Black poodle with gray spaghetti art hair. Fine Quality China Company. Made in Japan. 3.75" tall. $25-35.

Opposite page:
Pink set of poodles. Mother is wearing a black-velvet, rhinestone-covered collar. The puppies are wearing gold-colored collars. Both mother and puppies have blue rhinestone eyes. Kreiss and Company. Made in Japan. Mother, 12" tall; sitting pup, 6.5" tall; laying pup, 4.5" tall. $150-185 set.

Blue poodle wears gold collar, sits on pink chair with gold accents, and holds gold cup and saucer. Kelvin Exclusives. Made in Japan. 5.5" tall. $25-40.

Gray poodle sits on his hind legs and wears a red cap. Thames Co. Made in Japan. 5" tall. $15-25.

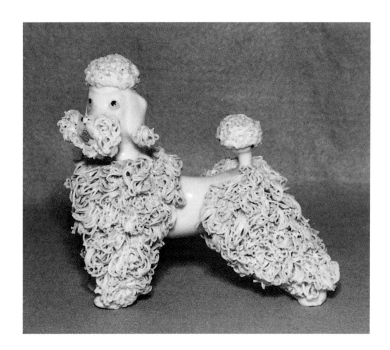

Pink poodle stands in show position. Kreiss and Company. Made in Japan. 4.5" tall. $15-25.

Black poodle with a lighter shade of black on tips of hair. Made in Japan. 2.75" tall. $15- 25.

Dark gray mother and pup with brown fur. Their eyes are white and black. Classica. Made in Japan. Mother: 4" tall, pup: 1.75" tall. $25-35 set.

Pink poodle with freckles and rhinestone eyes. Fur is highlighted with gold glitter. Kreiss and Company. Made in Japan. 3.75" tall. $15-25.

Pink poodle wears black sunglasses and black bow tie with rcd dots, gold highlights on fur. Original Arnart Creations. Made in Japan #7555. 5" tall. $25-35.

Gray poodle with gold collar stands on hind legs. Made in Japan. 6.5" tall. $18-25.

Two golden orange pups. Made in Japan. 3" tall. $15-20 each.

White poodle with black and yellow eyes. Made in Japan. 4.5" tall. $15-25.

Sitting, gray poodles wear gold collars, yellow and black eyes. Napco. Made in Japan #3627. Large: 4" tall. Small: 3.5" tall. **$25-35 set.**

White poodle with painted-black toenails and eyes. Made in Japan. 3" tall. $15-25.

Black pup planter. Fine Quality Japan. Made in Japan. 2.75" tall. $15-25.

Pink poodle with black collar and silver rhinestones, his body accented with gold. His eyes are blue and black. Lefton. Made in Japan. 4.75" tall. $18-25.

Pink poodle with gold collar and yellow and black eyes. Made in Japan. 3.5" long, 4" tall. $25-35.

Pink poodle with gold collar and aqua-blue rhinestone eyes. His fur is glittered with gold. Kreiss and Company. Made in Japan. 5.5" tall. $30-45.

White poodle with pups. All dogs wear gold collars and have blue eyes and black fur spotted with gold. Made in Japan. Mom, 4.5" tall; pups, 2" tall. $35-55 set.

White mother and puppies with gold collars and gold-tipped fur. Mother wears a hat with multi-colored flowers and the puppies have pink roses on their heads. Arnart Creations. Made in Japan. Mother, 4.75" tall; pups: 2.25" tall. $30-40 set.

Pink poodle mother wears an orchid; the whole family has blue, white, and black eyes and gold-accented fur. Lefton. Made in Japan. Mother: 5" tall. Pups: 2.5" tall. $23-50 set.

Pink poodles with blue eyes. Relco. Made in Japan. Mother, 3.5" x 4"; pups, 2" tall. $20-35 set.

Pink poodle with two pups. Take a close look at their faces. See the fine detail the artist has achieved with a lifelike expression in the eyes. Kreiss and Company. Made in Japan. Mother, 8" tall; pups, 4" tall. $90-120 set.

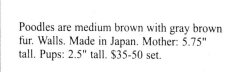

Poodles are medium brown with gray brown fur. Walls. Made in Japan. Mother: 5.75" tall. Pups: 2.5" tall. $35-50 set.

Light pink poodle with dark-pink hair and two pups. Eyes are blue rhinestones. Kreiss and Company. Made in Japan. Mother, 7" tall; pups, 3.5" tall. $95-120 set.

Pink poodle with pups. Their eyes are green rhinestones. Kreiss and Company. Made in Japan. Mother, 7.75" tall; pups: 2.75" tall. $35-50 set.

White poodle with two puppies. All have blue and black eyes, gold collars, and gold highlights on fur. Kreiss and Company. Made in Japan. Mother, 5.75" tall; pups, 2.5" tall. $25-40 set.

Pink poodle with pups, blue-green rhinestone eyes. Kreiss and Company. Made in Japan. Mother; 7" tall, pups, 3.5" tall. $90-120 set.

Pink poodle wearing blue bonnet accented with pink and green flowers. Puppies' and mother's eyes are blue and black. Gold collars and gold fur. Arnart Creations original. Made in Japan. Mother, 6.5" tall; pups, 2" tall. $25-40 set.

Opposite page:
White poodle with two puppies, gold-trimmed fur. Kreiss and Company. Made in Japan. Mother, 4.75" tall; pups, 2.5" tall. $20-38 set.

Blue poodle and pups with black and yellow eyes. Mother has green and white flowers across her head. Kreiss and Company. Made in Japan. Mother, 6.5" tall; pups, 3" and 2" tall. $25-35 set.

Large poodle with puppies, all wearing hats with pink flowers and gold-tipped fur. Made in Japan. Mother, 8.5" tall; pups, 2.75" tall. $25-40 set.

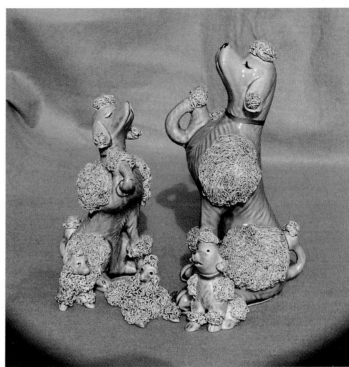

This is a complete family of canines. What a wonderful find. All dogs are wearing gold collars. Lefton. Made in Japan. Mother, 5.5" tall; pups, 2.75" and 1.75" tall. $45-70 set.

White poodle with two puppies; green scarf, and black eyes. Walls. Made in Japan. Mother, 5" tall; pups; 2.5" tall. $28-35 set.

Pink poodle set. Mother stands on hind legs with her pups by her side. They all have gold collars and black and brown eyes. Their fur is accented with pink roses. Kreiss and Company. Made in Japan. Mother, 5.5" tall; pups, 2.75" and 2" tall. $27-40 set.

Pink poodle in bonnet with pink and green flowers. Her black collar has silver rhinestones. Her eyes are blue and black. The puppies' bonnets have a single flower. Lefton. Made in Japan. #KB80550. Mother, 4.5" tall; pups, 2.5" tall. $25-40 set.

White poodle family with blue fur, blue-green rhinestone eyes, and white plastic beads around their necks. Mother has black collar with gold. Kreiss and Company. Made in Japan. Mother, 7" tall; pups, 3.5" tall. $90-120 set.

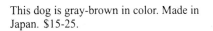

This dog is gray-brown in color. Made in Japan. $15-25.

23

White Scottie poodle with blue tam, yellow pompom, and yellow flowers. Orange and black eyes. Made in Japan. $15-25.

White Scottie poodle wearing a red tam with white, red, and blue pompom. Red collar and tam are accented with blue X's. Napco. Made in Japan. 5.5" tall. $18-28.

Large poodle wearing blue and yellow tam; small poodle wearing green and yellow tam. Royal. Made in Japan. Large, 6" tall; small, 4" tall. Large, $25-35; small, $20-30.

Blue poodle with yellow and black eyes. His tam is dark blue with a yellow pompom on top. Gold-painted collar. Hand Painted Royal Japan. Made in Japan. 3.5" tall. $18-25.

White poodle with black eyes. Sold for .39 cents new. Made in Japan. 2" tall, 3.75" long. $15 -20.

These pink poodles have lifelike faces. One is a little larger than the other. Kreiss and Company. Made in Japan. 4.5" x 3.5". $25-35 each.

Cream poodle with bow in hair sits on brown, blue, and pink pillow. Her fur is accented with black, her eyes are blue. Made in Japan. 6.5" tall. $20-30.

Pink poodle with nose full of freckles. Eyes are black with silver rhinestones. Kreiss and Company. Made in Japan. 8" tall. $35-45.

Reddish brown poodle carrying a yellow basket of multi-colored flowers, with a blue bow on handle. His collar is gold with a red bow. Thames Company. Made in Japan. 4.5" tall. $22-30.

This poodle wears a green-orange party hat with green dots and orange tassel in back. Made in Japan. 5.5" tall. $25-35.

This poodle has a purple and yellow flower on top of his head. His eyes and lips are brown, his tongue pink. Made in Japan. 5" tall. $18-25.

This dog is reddish brown in color and has a pattern etched into his body. Wales. Made in Japan. 4.5" x 5.5". $16-35.

Pair of pink poodle salt and pepper shakers. Eyes are blue and black and they wear gold collars. Numbered 104. Made in Japan. 3.5" tall. $35-50 pair.

White poodle with black eyes. Made in Japan. 2.5" tall. $15-20.

Set of poodles. Mom wears a black collar accented with clear rhinestones, has clear rhinestone eyes. Pups have gold collars and blue and black eyes. Made in Japan. Mom, 5.5" tall; pups, 2" tall. $35-45 set.

This pink poodle sports a velvet collar studded with silver rhinestones. Silver rhinestones are also used for his eyes. Lefton. Made in Japan. 4.75" tall, 3" long. $18-36.

This dog's fur is cut more like pieces of coleslaw than spaghetti. Napco. Made in Japan. 5.25" tall. $25-40.

White pup with black and yellow eyes. Made in Japan. 4" tall. $15-25.

Pink poodle with pink roses nestled in white fur. Her eyes are brown and black. Kreiss and Company. Made in Japan. 6" tall. $25-45.

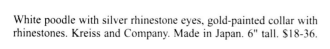

White poodle with silver rhinestone eyes, gold-painted collar with rhinestones. Kreiss and Company. Made in Japan. 6" tall. $18-36.

Black Scottie poodle with blue and yellow tam, gold collar. Napco. Made in Japan. 4.5" tall. $20-35.

Black poodle, "The Duchess," has yellow and black eyes and red tam accented with yellow and black. Napco. Made in Japan. 6" tall. $20-30.

Pair of black Scottie poodles. Their tams are blue with yellow pompoms, their collars are blue, their eyes are black and orange. Royal Japan. Made in Japan. 4.5" tall. 3.5" tall. $20-30 each.

This poodle is two-tone brown and is wearing a black bow tie with red polka dots. Relco. Made in Japan. 5.5" tall. $20-35.

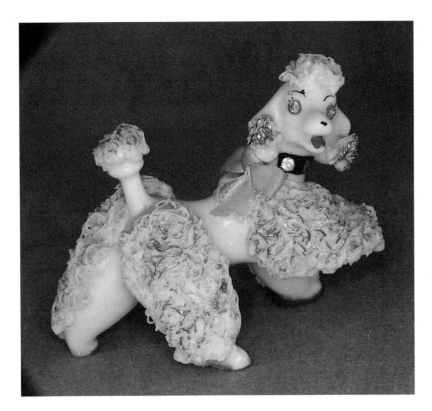

This poodle is white with a black collar and silver rhinestones. He has a cloth bow around his neck, silver rhinestone eyes, and gold accents. Napco. Made in Japan. 3.5" x 3.5". $20-30.

Mother poodle with litter; all are blue with gold collars and have orange and black eyes. Napco. Made in Japan. 4" x 4.5". $25-35.

This poodle is white with gray-green spaghetti fur. Made in Japan. 3.75" x 5.75". $25-35.

White poodle wears gold collar and has brown and black eyes. Made in Japan. 3.25" tall. $20-35.

Pink poodle wears aqua collar with silver rhinestones. Fur is gold tipped. Lipper and Mann. Made in Japan. 3.5" x 3". $20-35.

White poodle with gold features and collar. Made in Japan. 6" x 5.25". $25-35.

Two-toned black poodle. Roses with green leaves crown the head and wrap around the neck. Clear rhinestone eyes. Made in Japan. 3.75" x 3". $18-25.

White poodle with silver rhinestone-studded black bow tie, four green-leafed roses and gold dots on top of his bonnet, and gold highlights on fur. Lefton #KB8055P. Made in Japan. 5" x 3". $30-45.

White poodle wears a green ball cap. Made in Japan. 3" x 5". $20-30.

Black and white dog wears a top hat. Made in Japan. 4" x 3.5". $20-35.

Black poodle wears black top hat and has pink tongue. "Patent Applied." Made in Japan. 2.75" tall. $20-35.

This dog has a fly on the right side of his nose. Lefton. Made in Japan. 3.5" x 4". $25-35.

This is a planter. The fly has rested on the nose of one pup while the other looks on. Lefton. Made in Japan. 4.5" tall. $30-40.

Yellow hat with red ribbon and very pink cheeks. Lefton. Made in Japan. 4" tall. $30-40.

White dog with black spots wears a green ball cap. Made in Japan. 3.5" x 3". $20-35.

White and brown dog with freckles and pink cheeks. Wales. Made in Japan. 4.5" x 5". $25-35.

Lion or poodle? His fur is gray and tipped in gold. Eyes are orange and black. Thames Company. Made in Japan. 4" tall. $25-35.

This pretty lady wears a pink bonnet and sports a yellow and black polka-dot bow tie. Relco. Made in Japan. 5.5" x 4.5". $25-35.

Male and female poodles chained together. Flowers on female are indicative of those used by Lefton. Males cap is yellow with red stripes. Lefton. Made in Japan. 4.5" x 2.5" and 3.5" x 3". $30-40 set.

This poodle wears a gold collar. Good example of spaghetti art work. Made in Japan. 2" x 2.125". $25-35.

This pup has a toothache, a tear on his cheek, and a fly on his forehead. Lefton. Registered U.S. Patent Office. #587. Made in Japan. 4.75" tall. $25-35.

This pup has a hurt tail, a fly on his rump, and a tear on his cheek. Lefton. Made in Japan. 2.75" tall. $25-35.

Brown and white pup with a fly on his nose, his arm in a red polka-dot sling, and a tear on his right cheek. Lefton. Made in Japan. 5" tall. $25-35.

Pup has a fly resting on his forehead and pink cheeks and freckles. Lefton. Made in Japan. 4.5" tall. $25-35.

This puppy finds the fly on her forehead very curious indeed. Her color is light brown and white. Her eyes are yellow and black. "Kelvin Exclusives." Made in Japan. 4.5" tall. $25-35.

This pup is brown and white with black and blue eyes. He's looking at the fly on his forehead. "Kelvin Exclusives." Made in Japan. 3.5" tall. $25-35.

This pup is brown and white. His eyes are crossed to look at the fly on the bridge of his nose. "Kelvin Exclusives." Made in Japan. 4.5" tall. $25-35.

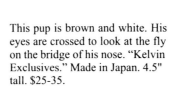

Brown and white pup wearing black hat with yellow band. Made in Japan. 3" tall. $25- 35.

Red and white pup with a pink bonnet trimmed in blue, a red flower, and green leaves. "Kelvin Exclusives." Made in Japan. 3" tall. $25-35.

Pink poodle with flowers on her head. She is adorned with lots of gold. Her eyes are blue and black. Pups have yellow and black eyes. Made in Japan. Mom, 6" tall; pups, 2.5" tall. $30-40 set.

Pink poodle with rose on top of head and gold collar. Pups have gold collars. Lefton. Made in Japan. Mom, 7" tall; pups, 1.5" tall. $20-30 set.

White poodle with purple tie carries a top hat and cane. Made in Japan. 5.5" tall. $20-35.

White poodle wears orange beret with green spots. Made in Japan. 2.5" tall. $20-30.

Dark brown poodle with blue rhinestone eyes. His lashes are long, black bristles. Pearls adorn the tip of his tail and his toes. There are rhinestones in his fur. Wales. Made in Japan. 4.5" tall. $30-45.

White poodle with pearls nestled in fur, a gold collar, and a beaded necklace with pink flowers around her neck. Made in Japan. 3.5" tall. $25-35.

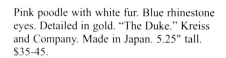

Pink poodle with white fur. Blue rhinestone eyes. Detailed in gold. "The Duke." Kreiss and Company. Made in Japan. 5.25" tall. $35-45.

Burgundy poodle with black eyes. Made in Japan. 4" tall. $25-35.

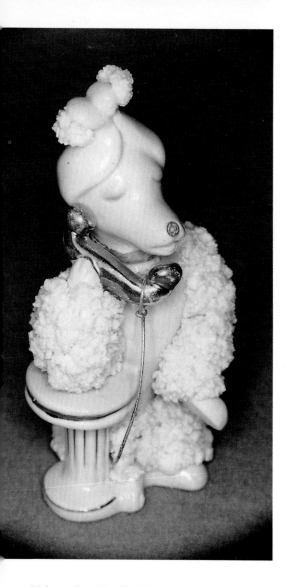

Black poodle and pup. Gold collars. Royal Japan. Made in Japan. Mother, 4" tall; pup, 1.75" tall. $35-50 set.

Pink poodle with white fur. Details including telephone are done in gold. "The Duchess." Kreiss and Company. Made in Japan. 5.25" tall. $35-45.

Light pink poodles. Eyes are black and orange. Royal Japan. Made in Japan. Standing, 5.5" tall; squatting, 3.75 tall. $25-35 each.

White poodle pup wears yellow hat with blue polka dots and red sash and a gold collar. Eyes are orange and black. Made in Japan. 3.75" tall. $25-35.

White poodle with pink umbrella. Made in Japan. 3" tall. $40-65.

White poodle holding umbrella. Her fur is spattered in gold and she's wearing a gold collar. Made in Japan. 3" tall. $40-65.

A set of three with silver rhinestone eyes and gold collars. Kreiss and Company. Made in Japan. Mother, 7.75" tall; pups, 4.5" and 3.5" tall. $40-55 set.

Mother and two pups. Their eyes are light brown and black and they wear gold collars. Napco. Made in Japan. 3.5" tall. $35-45 set.

Dark pink poodle with black eyes. Royal Ceramics. Made in Japan. 3.5" tall. $25-35.

Gray poodle with black eyes. Royal Japan. Made in Japan. 3" x 5". $30-40.

Pair of pink poodle salt and pepper shakers wearing black berets' and black bow ties. Their eyes are yellow and black. Made in Japan. 3.75" tall. $45-65 pair.

White poodle has gray fur and it is covered with gold. Thames Company. Made in Japan. 5" tall. $30-40.

White poodle with pink tint on fur. The fur is thick in width and resembles coleslaw rather than spaghetti decoration. Eyes are yellow and black. Napco. Made in Japan. 5" tall. $25-40.

Pink poodle accented in gold wears a headdress and carries a bouquet of multi-colored flowers. Napco. Made in Japan. 4.5" tall. $35-45.

Pink poodle sporting the most popular poodle cut. Carrying a newspaper marked "Times." Red collar with silver rhinestones. Lefton. Made in Japan. 4.75" tall. $30-45.

Pink poodle wearing sunglasses with clear rhinestones in corners. Black bow tie with red polka dots. Gold accents on fur. Classic. Made in Japan. 5.5" tall. $35-45.

This poodle is white and trimmed in gold and wears black sunglasses with rhinestones and a black bow tie with red polka dots. Classic Inc. Made in Japan. 4.5" tall. $35-45.

Pink poodle with a white gardenia in her hair. Her fur is highlighted in gold. Enesco Imports. Made in Japan. 4.5" tall. $35-45.

Reddish brown poodle with gold collar and painted eyes. Classica Inc. Made in Japan. 5" long. $28-40.

This poodle is white and trimmed in gold and wears black sunglasses with rhinestones and a black bow tie with red polka dots. Classic Inc. Made in Japan. 4.5" tall. $35-45.

This guy's tam is red with blue marks and a red, white, and blue pompom. "Kelvin Exclusives." Made in Japan. 4" tall. $25-35.

Planter with a black and white pup with rosy cheeks and a shoe to chew. Kelvin Exclusives. Made in Japan. 4.75" tall. $25-35.

This dog is gray and wears a red beret. Made in Japan. 5.75" tall. $35-45.

This poodle's fur is tipped in silver and he has black and white eyes. Lefton. Made in Japan. 8.5" tall. $28-40.

This poodle is very black with pink roses. Green rhinestones accented with white make the eyes very bright. Kreiss and Company. Made in Japan. 8" tall. $25-35.

Black poodle with yellow eyes. Red collar with clear rhinestones. Lefton. Made in Japan. 4" tall. $30-40.

Blue poodle detailed in gold. Walls. Registered U.S. Patent Office. Made in Japan. 8" tall. $35-50.

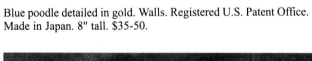

Yellow poodle with gold eyes and collar. Walls. Made in Japan. Registered U.S. Patent Office. 5.5" tall. $35-50.

Standing yellow poodle trimmed in gold. Walls. Registered U.S. Patent Office. Made in Japan. 6" tall. $35-50.

White poodle with black and brown eyes, wearing a gold collar. Made in Japan. 3.25" tall. $15-25.

White poodle and pup wearing red polka-dotted collars. The shape is unusual. Made in Japan. Mother, 3" tall; pups, 2.25" tall. $20-30 set.

Gray poodle with red polka-dot beret and matching bow tie. Black and yellow eyes. Made in Japan. 3.5" tall. $20-30.

Large pink poodle with a very large white bow tie with black dots. Eyes painted blue and black. Red tongue. Fur is accented in gold. Lefton. Made in Japan. 6.5" x 6.5". $45-60.

Poodle night light and aromatic dispenser. Pour perfume oil into the indentation on top of the hat and, when the light is on, the oil heats and emits a pleasant aroma. He has blue rhinestone eyes and gold bow tie and holds a bouquet of roses in his mouth. Made in Japan. 6.25" tall. $45-65.

White poodle wearing red beany cap and gold collar. Thames Company. Made in Japan. 5.5" tall. $30-45.

Pink poodle with silver glitter and silver rhinestone eyes. Napco. Made in Japan. 4.5" x 4". $25-35.

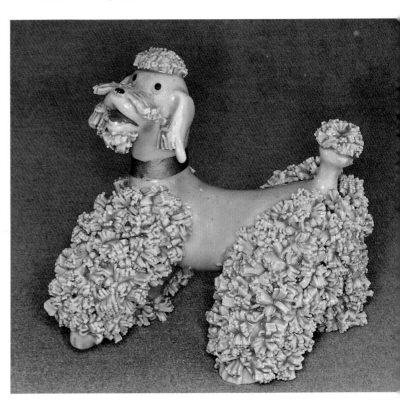

Standard dark gray poodle. Made in Japan. 4.5" tall. $35-50.

White poodle with green fur and multi-colored flowers. Eyes are brown and black. This poodle's coloring is very unusual. Thames Company. Made in Japan. 6" tall. $35-50.

Blue poodle wearing gold collar with yellow and black eyes. Napco. Made in Japan. 4.5" x 4" long. $25-35.

Brown Scottie poodle. "The Duke." His tam is red with blue squares and yellow dots. His collar matches the tam. Napco. Made in Japan. 5.5" tall. $25-35.

Burgundy pup. This color is very unusual. His fur is accented by white. Eyes are orange and black. Made in Japan. 3" tall. $30-40.

Black poodle wearing red glasses and cap. He's holding a white walking cane. His fur is an off-color brown. Wales. Made in Japan. 6" tall. $38-45.

Black poodle playing a flute. His fur is rusty brown. Napco. Made in Japan. 5.25" tall. $30-40.

Pink poodle with dark pink fur wears a red beanie, red glasses, and a gold collar. His eyes are brown and black. Wales. Made in Japan. 4" tall. $30-45.

Pepper shaker pup has red hair, white body, and rosy cheeks. Lefton. Made in Japan. 4" tall. $30-40.

This dog is a small planter. He's looking back at his bandaged tail or maybe the fly on his hip. Lefton. Made in Japan. 2.5" x 5". $25-40.

Salt shaker dog has black hair, freckles, and rosy cheeks. Lefton. Made in Japan. 4" tall. $30-40.

White poodle planter. Blue and green rhinestones on planter. The poodle has gold highlights on fur and wears a gold collar. Lefton. Made in Japan. 5" x 4.5". $35-50.

This blue poodle is holding onto a cigarette caddy. He's highlighted in gold and has black eyes. Lefton. Made in Japan. #KB40205. 4.25" tall. $35-50.

Set of light blue ashtrays. These ashtrays are trimmed in gold and so are the cute little poodles on top. Lefton. Made in Japan. $30-40 each.

Pink poodle bank. Blue rhinestone eyes. Ribbon around neck. Kreiss and Company. Made in Japan. 8" tall. $50-75.

Poodle night light. Trimmed in gold. Made in Japan. 6" tall. $40-50.

White poodle planter with gold painted leaves. Royal Ceramics. Made in Japan. 4.5" x 3.5". $35-50.

This poodle has a black collar with silver rhinestones. Her eyes are silver rhinestones and she is trimmed in gold. Made in Japan. 3" x 2.75". $35-50.

Black poodle planter. Eyes are black and light brown. Lefton. Made in Japan. 4.75" tall. $35-50.

These poodles are different than most. They are not marked and have rhinestones in their eyes. Made in Japan. 6.75" tall. $25-40 each.

Bride dog with pearl-studded veil and fur, eyelashes, pink bow, white fur, blue rhinestone eyes, and a collar of tiny pearls. Wales. Made in Japan. Registered U.S. Patent Office. $35-50.

White poodle with gold collar and black eyes. Made in Japan. 2.5" tall. $25-40.

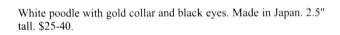

White poodle planter cart, blue and black eyes, gold collar and gold accents on cart, and red toenails. Napco. Made in Japan. 6" tall. $35-50.

This piece is very unusual. It is a pin cushion and scissor holder. Pink and trimmed in gold. Eyes are blue and black. California Creations by Bradley. Made in Japan. 7.5" tall. $45-60.

Pink poodle holding onto a basket with black roses in two of the corners and gold accents. The dog's eyes are blue and black. Boutique by Essy. New York. Made in Japan #897. 4.75" tall. $35-50.

White poodle matchstick holder. Eyes are black, brown and white. There is a pink cloth bow on his forehead. Enesco Imports. Made in Japan. 5.5" tall. $35-50.

Pink poodle planter cart. The poodle is wearing a black beret and is dashed in gold. The planter is accented in gold. Lefton. Made in Japan. 4.75" x 7". $35-50.

Pink poodle planter. Poodle has gold highlights on fur and clear rhinestone eyes. The planter has two white flowers trimmed in gold. Lefton. Made in Japan. 5" x 6". $40-50.

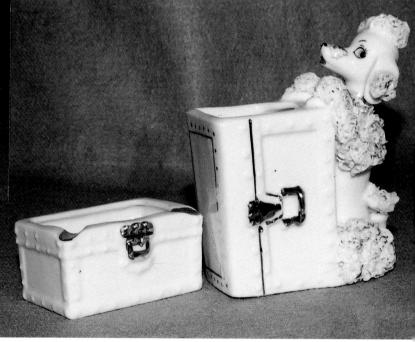

This pink poodle is a cigarette holder and ashtray. Lefton. Made in Japan. 4.25" x 3". $40-55.

White donkey planter with pink raised flowers on side. His hat has two pink roses on front of brim. Spaghetti work is very three-dimensional and sprinkled with gold. The basket has woven appearance. His eyes are black and blue. Lefton. Made in Japan. 4.5" x 5.25". $40-55.

Pink poodle planter cart. Wheels are accented in gold. Lefton. Made in Japan. 5" x 7". $35-50.

This poodle is sitting in a crown studded with multi-colored rhinestones. Blue stones in eyes. The poodle and crown are accented in gold. Velvet sash across shoulders. Kreiss and Company. Made in Japan. 6.5" tall. $30-50.

Pink poodle planter wearing black beret and black belt. Planter is trimmed in gold. Lefton. Made in Japan. 4.75" x 7". $35-50.

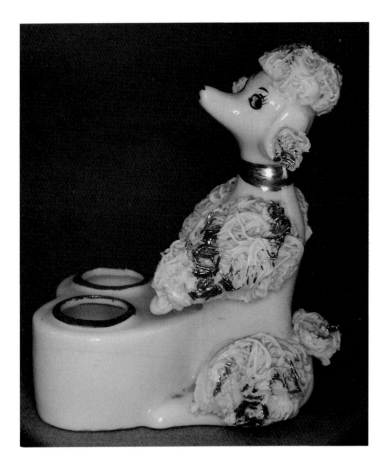

White poodle lipstick holder. Poodle and lipstick holder are accented in gold. Eyes are blue and black. Lefton. Made in Japan. 4.5" tall. $35-50.

Pink poodle vase. The fur on the poodle and the vase are accented in gold. Her eyes are black and brown. Thames Company. Made in Japan. 4.75" tall. $35-50.

This flower vase and poodle are trimmed in gold. This piece is in excellent shape. Lefton. Registered U.S. Patent Office. Made in Japan #1633. 5.5" tall. $35-55.

Gray-brown poodle trinket holder. Blue and black eyes. Hand Painted Tilso. Made in Japan. 4.5" tall. $35-50.

Soft blue poodle container with lid. The container is trimmed in gold and green flowers. Thames Company. Made in Japan. 5.75" x 3.5". $35-50.

This poodle is very crazed and shows a lot of wear and tear. Classica Incorporated. Made in Japan. 4.5" x 5". $35-45.

Small log planter accented only by pup perched on top. Lefton. Made in Japan. 5" x 6". $30-45.

Pink poodle with basket vase. Basket has flowers around rim. Lefton. Made in Japan. 4" tall. $35-50.

Pink poodle cart planter. Black beanie and white polka-dot tie. Wearing cool black shades with rhinestones in corners. Gold accents on cart. Walls. Made in Japan. $35-45.

Small log planter with brown-tan poodle attached. Lefton. Made in Japan. $35-45.

White poodle with pup. Eyes are blue. Collar gold. Fur is also accented with gold. Lefton. Made in Japan. Mom, 3.5" x 4.75"; pup, 3" x 2.75". $35-45 set.

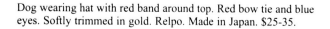

Dog wearing hat with red band around top. Red bow tie and blue eyes. Softly trimmed in gold. Relpo. Made in Japan. $25-35.

Cowboy doggie with ten-gallon hat, yellow polka-dot scarf, and off-white spaghetti art on white body. Lefton. Made in Japan. 3.5" x 2.5". $30-40.

Poodle wearing wedding veil. Her bow tie is pink with black polka dots. Relco. Made in Japan. 5.5" tall. $30-40.

Brown and white dog wears a yellow bonnet and is trimmed in blue and pink with blue flowers. Lefton. Made in Japan. 3.5" x 3". $30-45.

Brown and white dog. What is unusual about this dog is that he has teeth. His upper lip is rolled back and his snoot is covered with freckles. Wales. Made in Japan. 2.5" x 4". $30-45.

Small white poodle with bonnet and single white rose. Speckled with gold. Lefton. Made in Japan. 2.75" x 2.75". $25-35.

White poodle holding basket of blue and pink roses with gold collar and black eyes. Lefton. Made in Japan #4372. $35-45.

White poodle. His handbag, umbrella, and bow tie are a deep purple. Polka dots are white. Relco. Made in Japan. 6" tall. $45-55.

White poodle pup with yellow and purple flower nestled on top of her head. Gold collar. Lefton. Made in Japan. 3" x 1.75". $25-35.

This white poodle has gold-tipped wings and holds a flute. Red collar with blue and black eyes. Relco. Made in Japan. 6" tall. $35-45.

This pair of dancing poodles are white with gold collars. Lefton. Made in Japan. 5.5" x 3.75". $40-50.

Small white poodle wears pink hat trimmed in multi-colored flowers. Her collar is pink. Relpo. Made in Japan. 3" x 2.75". $30-40.

Pink porcelain pup with gold accents on fur. Her collar is gold. Napco. Made in Japan #1G2776. 4" tall. $30-45.

Pink poodle with blue rhinestone eyes. Kreiss and Company. Made in Japan. 4.5" x 2.5". $35-45.

Mother poodle with her pup. These white poodles are trimmed in gold. West Pac. Made in Japan. Mom, 6.25" tall; pup, 2" tall. $45-55 set.

Mother poodle with her pups. They are brushed in gold. The pups have a single pink rose on top of their heads. Mom wears a bonnet trimmed in gold and pink roses. Lefton. Made in Japan. Mom, 4" x 3.75"; pup right, 2.5" tall; pup left, 2" tall. $55-65 set.

Mother and pup poodles wearing pink hats and gold collars. Their fur is blue. The pup is wearing a pink bow tie. Kreiss and Company. Made in Japan. Mom,5.5" tall; pup, 3" tall. $55-65 set.

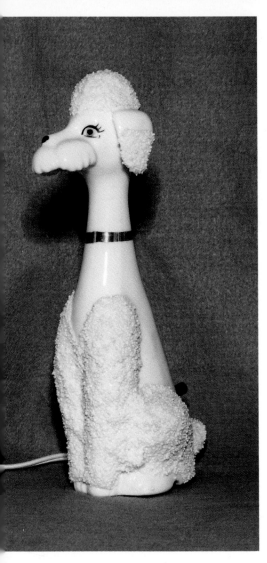

White poodle night light wearing gold collar. Lefton. Made in Japan. 8" tall. $50-65.

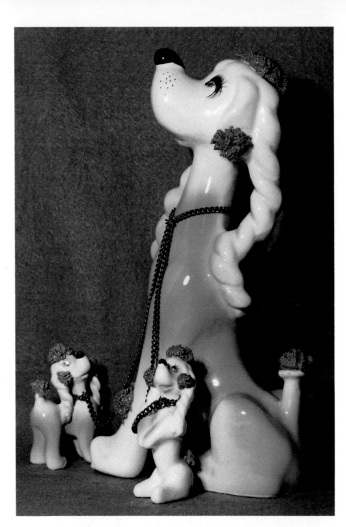

Family of white poodles with blue accents on bodies and blue spaghetti on heads, tails, and ears. Kreiss and Company. Made in Japan. Mom, 8.25" tall; pups, 2.5" and 3" tall. $45-60 set.

Family of white poodles with pink spaghetti on their legs, ears, and tails. They all have red rhinestone eyes. Kreiss and Company. Made in Japan. Mom, 7.5" tall; pups, 3.5" tall. $45-60 set.

Poodle night light, room deodorizer. This guy's hat is concave to hold cologne so when the light is on the cologne heats up and permeates your room. Lefton. Made in Japan. 6" tall. $55-65.

Pair of white poodles. Mister on left has a spaghetti beard and eyebrows. The lady on the right is wearing a pink derby and gold collar. Relpo. Made in Japan. Both, 2.25" tall. $20-25 each.

This pretty poodle has red tongue and collar. . His fur is accented in gold and his eyes are silver rhinestones. Napco. Made in Japan. 4.75" x 3.25". $25-35.

Sitting poodle with pearl earrings and necklace. Her eyelashes are black and very long. She has blue rhinestone eyes. Napco. Made in Japan. 5.75" tall. $25-35.

This poodle is white with gold accents and his collar is red with silver rhinestones. Lipper and Mann Creations. Made in Japan. 4.75" tall. $25-35.

This poodle perfumer night light carries a
blue basket of pink roses and wears a pink
bonnet. Lefton. Made in Japan. 6.75" tall.
$50-60.

This poodle appears to be obeying a
command. He has clear rhinestone eyes and a
red collar with clear rhinestones. His fur is
accented in gold. Lefton. Made in Japan.
5.5" tall. $25-35.

These dinner bells are examples of how the
art was used. Rhinestones and gold trim add
a radiant glow to the pieces. Lefton. Made in
Japan. 5" tall. $20-30 each.

These dogs only have spaghetti applications on their legs and tail
tips. They all have black and blue eyes. Lefton. Made in Japan.
Mom, 4.5" x 2.75"; pups, 2.25" x 1.5". $35-45 set.

White and gold poodle cart accented with pink flowers. Lefton. Made in Japan. 3" x 5". $35-45.

White standard poodle tipped in gold. Tilso. Made in Japan. 4" x 4.5". $18-36.

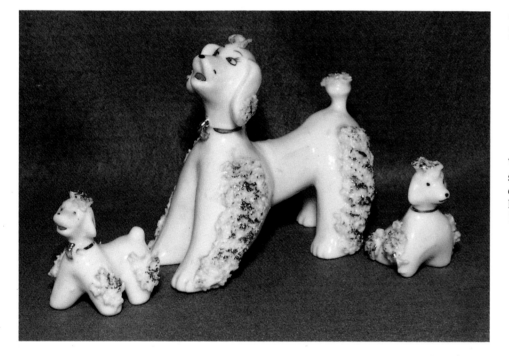

White poodles dashed in gold. Large dog has single pink rose on top of her head. Their collars are gold. Original Arnart creation. Made in Japan. Mom, 3.75" x 3.75"; pups, 1.75" tall. $35-45 set.

Pink poodle set. Napco. Made in Japan. Mom, 3.5" x 3.25"; pups, 2" tall. $45-55 set.

French poodle with gold hat and collar and blue eyes. Kreiss and Company. Made in Japan. 5.25" x 3". $25-35.

White Scottie wearing gold collar. Wales. Made in Japan. 4.5" x 5.5". $25-35.

Pink poodle wearing hat with blue flowers trimmed in gold. California Creations by Bradley. Made in Japan. 7.5" tall. $25-35.

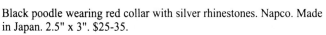

Black poodle wearing red collar with silver rhinestones. Napco. Made in Japan. 2.5" x 3". $25-35.

White dog playing drum. Made in Japan. 3.75" tall. $25-35.

White poodle playing yellow bugle. He's wearing a gold collar and has black and gold colored eyes. His fur is highlighted in gold. Wales. Made in Japan. 5.75" tall. $30-40.

White dog playing tuba. Made in Japan. 3.75" tall. $25-35.

Gray dog is playing the drum. Thames. Made in Japan. 4.5" tall. $25-35.

Pink poodle playing horn. Thames. Made in Japan. 4.75" tall. $30-40.

White dog playing accordion. Gold accents on accordion. Made in Japan. 4.75" tall. $30-40.

Pink poodle playing tuba. His eyes are clear rhinestones. He is trimmed in gold. Made in Japan #3011. 3.75" tall. $30-40.

White poodle playing violin. His eyes are brown and black. The violin is trimmed in gold. Thames Company. Made in Japan. 5" tall. $30-40.

White dog playing cello. His eyes are black and his cello is trimmed in gold. Made in Japan. 2.75" tall. $30-40.

Gray poodle playing red flute. Thames Company. Made in Japan. 5.5" tall. $30-40.

Gray dog playing red-and-gray drum. His eyes are black and white. Thames Company. Made in Japan. 6" tall. $30-40.

Black poodle with yellow eyes. Sunsco. Made in Japan. 3.5" x 3". $25-35.

Pink and white poodle set. Eyes are blue rhinestones. Kreiss and Company. Made in Japan. Mom, 6.75" x 7.25"; pups, 3.5" x 2". $100-125 set.

Left poodle off-white with gold collar. Poodle on right is light pink with blue collar. Made in Japan. Left, 4.25" tall; right, 3.5" tall. $20-30 each.

Pink poodle with white pearls on top of her head. Her eyes are black and blue. Kreiss and Company. Made in Japan. 3.5" x 5". $25-35.

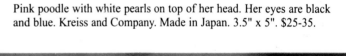

This pair of poodles is white with blue rhinestone eyes for mom and painted eyes for pup. Kreiss and Company. Made in Japan. Mom, 8.5" x 9"; pup, 3.75" x 4.5". $65-80 pair.

Gray poodle with spaghetti art on tip of tail and head. Kreiss and Company. Made in Japan. 3" x 2.75". $25-35.

Pink poodle with cane and top hat. Bow tie is accented with clear rhinestones. His eyes are blue and black. Kreiss and Company. Made in Japan. 5.75" tall. $30-40.

Mom is wearing a bonnet held onto her head with a blue bandana. She has blue and black eyes and a single rose on top of her hat. The pups eyes are blue and black. Kreiss and Company. Made in Japan. Mom, 5.75" tall; pups, 2.5" tall. $35-45 set.

Pink poodles with gold collars. Mom's eyes are blue and black. Pup's eyes are blue. Lefton. Made in Japan. Mom, 4" tall; pups, 2" tall. $45-55 set.

Pink terrier with silver rhinestones for eyes. He's wearing a black tie and has a frown on his face. Norcrest Fine China. Made in Japan. 4.75" x 3". $25-30.

Scottie dog wearing black top hat. He's sticking his tongue out at something. Kreiss and Company. Made in Japan. 3.25" x 3.5". $25-35.

Brown poodle playing bass. His instrument, collar, and tongue are highlighted in red. Made in Japan. 2.75" tall. $25-35.

White poodle with multi-colored flowers on her head, feet, collar, and ears. Her collar is gold. Lefton. Made in Japan. 4.75" long. $25-35.

Black and white pup with brown hat, gold ribbon, and red tongue. Made in Japan. 8.5" tall. $20-30.

Set of white poodles. Mom is wearing a bonnet with a cluster of flowers on top. The pups have gold collars and blue eyes. Arnart Creations . Made in Japan. Mom, 5" tall; pups, 2.25" tall. $45-55 set.

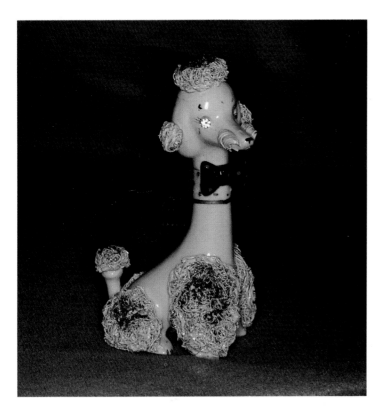

Pink poodle with black and red bow tie, clear rhinestone eyes, and gold collar. Made in Japan. 5.75" tall. $25-35.

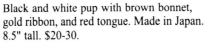

Black and white pup with brown bonnet, gold ribbon, and red tongue. Made in Japan. 8.5" tall. $20-30.

Pink poodle with red collar embossed with clear rhinestones. Lefton. Made in Japan. 5" x 4.5". $30-40.

This pretty white poodle is carrying a gold watering can to water her flowers. She has a gold collar and green eyes. Napco. Made in Japan. 4" tall. $35-45.

Pink poodle wearing hat with pink flowers. She has a black collar with clear rhinestones. California Creations by Bradley. Made in Japan. 7.5" tall. $25-35.

This poodle is playing cymbals and a drum. Thames Company. Made in Japan. 5" tall. $30-40.

Black poodle with white flowers on head, paws, and under chin.
Napco. Made in Japan. 2.25" x 3". $25-35.

Pair of black poodles with gold collars.
Made in Japan. Large, 6.5" x 5.5" long;
small, 3.75" x 4.25". $25-35 each.

Gray poodle. Pink collar has pink rhinestones. Made in Japan. 7.75"
x 10". $35-45.

Pink poodle with her litter. Mother's eyes are black and blue. Her fur is dotted with gold. Napco Ceramics. Made in Japan #164179. Mother, 5" tall; pups, 2.5" tall. $35-45 set.

White poodle with pink rose on right shoulder, yellow and black eyes, and gold highlights on fur. Made in Japan. 5.75" x 3.5". $25-35.

White poodle with pink rose under her chin and yellow and black eyes. Made in Japan. 5.5" x 4.125". $25-35.

White poodle with pink rose under her chin, yellow and black eyes, and gold highlights on fur. Made in Japan. 4.5" x 5.5". $25-35.

Blue dog with gold collar. Made in Japan. 1.25" x 1.5". $20-30.

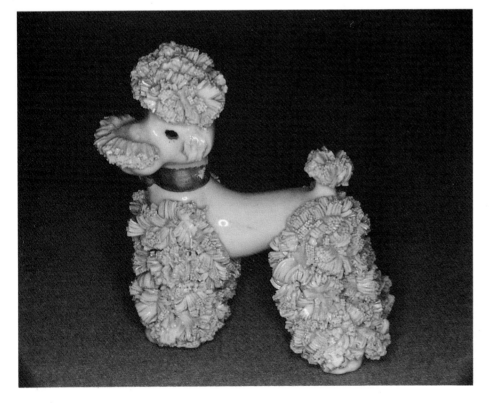

Pink poodle with gold collar. Made in Japan. 3" x 2.5". $20-30.

Black poodle with gold collar. Made in Japan. 2.25" x 4.5". $25-35.

Black poodle with gold and black collar. Yellow and black eyes. Made in Japan. 3" x 2.75". $25-35.

Black poodle with black and gold collar. Yellow and black eyes. Made in Japan. 3" x 2.75". $25-35.

Pink poodles. Their eyes are green rhinestones. Their fur was tipped in gold and glitter was applied. Kreiss and Company. Made in Japan. Mom, 5" tall; pups, 3.75" tall. $18-25 each.

White poodle wears a gold collar. His eyes are painted black and brown. His mustache is much bolder than the gold on his fur. Made in Japan. 5.75" tall. $20-30.

White poodle with silver rhinestone eyes. Kreiss and Company. Made in Japan. 8" tall. $25-35.

These black pups bodies are made of red clay. Ceramic eyes are white and brown. Fine Quality Japan. Made in Japan. Large, 9" head to tail; small, 4" head to tail. Large: $20-30. Small: $15-25.

This Scottie is wearing an orange jacket with red stripes. His tam is red with an orange pompom. Kreiss and Company. Made in Japan. 5.5" tall. $25-35.

Set of gray poodles sitting on white lamp. Made in Los Angeles, California U.S.A. By Visun Company. Mom, 4" tall; pups: 2.25" tall; lamp, 12" tall. $75-100.

Pink poodle with nose full of freckles. Eyes are black with silver rhinestones. Kreiss and Company. Made in Japan. 8" tall. $45-65.

Cat perfumer night light wears gold bow tie and a pink hat with a single rose. She is dusted with gold and has green rhinestone eyes. Lefton. Made in Japan. 6" tall. $55-65.

Other Animals

Family of pink elephants. Mom wears a white bonnet with red rose and a pink polka-dot bow tie. The babies have a single pink rose on their heads. Wales. Made in Japan. Mom, 5" x 2.5"; pups, 2.5" tall. $45-55 set.

Black horse with gold hoofs. His mane and tail are white spaghetti. Napco. Made in Japan. 5.5" x 5.75". $35-45.

White horse with blue flowers wrapped around hoofs. Napco. Made in Japan. 5.25" x 5.75". $35-45.

Dark green horse with light green spaghetti. Napco. Made in Japan. 5.5" x 5.75". $35-45.

Zebra with spaghetti on mane, tail, and hoofs. Napco. Made in Japan. 6.5" tall. $30-40.

Pink monkey wears blue flowers, gold collar, and gold nails. He has black and blue eyes. Enesco. Made in Japan. 5" tall. $20-30.

White Elephant beating a drum and playing cymbals. He wears a gold halo with a very happy expression on his face. "Hand Painted Lenville China. Ardalt Verithin. Made in Japan." 5" tall. $30-40.

Pink pony trimmed with white spaghetti art. She has green rhinestone eyes and pink and blue flowers on her neck and forehead. Kreiss and Company. Made in Japan. 5.25" x 5.75". $25-35.

Pink pig piggy bank carries a coat of arms. He has rhinestone eyes. The coins are dropped into his helmet. Spaghetti work adorns black cape and tip of toes. Gold used to accent color. Lefton. Made in Japan #YU9046. 7" tall. $25-35.

Rabbit wearing bonnet with pink flowers. Bunnies have blue eyes and pink roses on top of their heads. Sealey. Made in Japan. Mom, 7.5" tall; pups,1.5" tall. $35-45 set.

Mama sheep with two lambs. She is wearing a blue bonnet with blue flowers. Gold highlights woven through their wool. Enesco. Made in Japan. 4.75" tall. $35-45 set.

I believe this to be a bear and her two cubs. A nice soft looking piece. Fun to look at. "Original Arnart Creation." Made in Japan #7836. Mom, 4" tall; pups, 2" tall. $35-45 set.

A happy mouse pulls a cart. His head is adorned with blue flowers. Lefton. Made in Japan. 5.25" x 4.5". $35-45.

White lamb with pink and gold accents. His eyes are blue and black. Original Arnart Creations. Made in Japan. 3.5" tall. $25-35.

White lamb with pink and gold accents. Left ear has three pink roses. Paws are gray. Original Arnart Creations. Made in Japan. 5.5" tall. $25-35.

White monkey with grin on his face. Napco. Made in Japan. 3" tall. $25-35.

Green stallion is ready to rumble. Made in Japan. 4.5" x 5.75". $35-45.

Now here's a jolly ole Santa. Good facial expression, and he's a planter. Spirit of Christmas. By Robyn. Patent Pending. Made in Japan. 8" tall. $30-40.

Holiday Figurines

Fourth of July angel bell. Spaghetti art on gown. Napco. Made in Japan 1956. 3" tall. $25-35.

Santa salt and pepper shakers. Napco. Made in Japan. 2.5" tall. $30-40 set.

Pair of salt and pepper Christmas angels. Holt Howard. Made in Japan 1958. 4.5" tall. $40-50 set.

Santa sitting in a boot. Spaghetti art is accented in gold. Napco. Made in Japan. 4.25" tall. $35-45.

Salt and pepper Santas. Napco. Made in Japan. 3" tall. $30-40 set.

Very colorful Christmas planter. Relpo. Made in Japan #496. 5" x 5". $45-55.

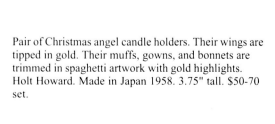

Pair of Christmas angel candle holders. Their wings are tipped in gold. Their muffs, gowns, and bonnets are trimmed in spaghetti artwork with gold highlights. Holt Howard. Made in Japan 1958. 3.75" tall. $50-70 set.

Jolly old Saint Nick piggy bank holding holly in his upraised hand. Relpo. Made in Japan. 6.25" x 4.5". $45-55.

This Santa has a very rosy face. He's holding a green stocking and white package. Lefton. Made in Japan. 4.5" tall. $30-40.

This Santa has rosy cheeks and carries a bag full of toys. Lefton. Made in Japan. 4.5" tall. $30-40.

Here's Santa coming out of a chimney. Very nice porcelain piece with real beard. Napco. Made in Japan. 6.5" tall. $45-55.

This Santa is carrying his knapsack while going for a walk. An Irice Import. Irving W. Rice and Company Inc. New York City. Made in Japan. 5" tall. $30-40.

Santa planter or candy holder? Napco. Made in Japan. 7" tall. $45-55.

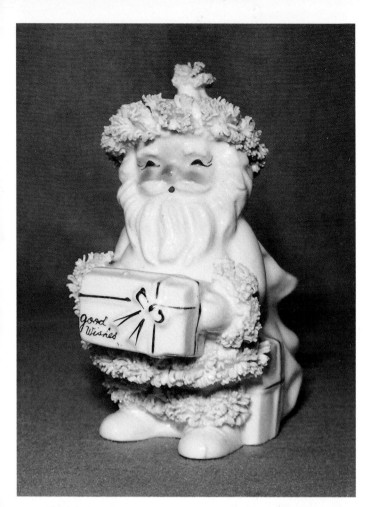

White Santa planter holding package. Spaghetti art on cap and jacket. Napco. Made in Japan #S268. 5" tall. $35-45.

Very colorful Santa planter holding package on upraised arm. Inarco. Made in Japan. 7" tall. $35-45.

This Christmas Angel is holding gold bells and a Christmas Tree. There were a series of these Christmas bells made. Lefton. Made in Japan. 4" tall. $30-40.

Christmas Angel. You can see her wings over
her right shoulder. Lefton. Made in Japan.
4.5" tall. $30-40.

Angel Bell carrying a hymn book and gold
bell. Spaghetti art trims robe and bonnet.
Lefton. Made in Japan. 4" tall. $30-40.

Choir Boy with green jacket, carrying a cake
with gold candle. There are pink flowers at
the base of the cake. The jacket is trimmed in
spaghetti artwork. Lefton. Made in Japan.
4.5" tall. $25-35.

Here's a real find! Santa coming out of a chimney holding a ballerina. Vcagco Ceramics. Made in Japan. 6" tall. $65-85.

Fairy princess with golden wings and crown. Heart shaped staff has multi-colored rhinestones. Her cape is trimmed in gold and rhinestones. Zall Design. Made in Japan. 4.75" tall. $35-45.

Angel bell. Very colorful. She's holding a plate in her right hand and a candle in her left. Napco. Made in Japan. 4" tall. $30-40.

Christmas planter. Hood shows spaghetti art around face. Lefton #1469. Made in Japan. 6.5" tall. $30-40.

Angel bearing gifts and treats. Napco #AX1703. Made in Japan. 7.5" tall. $35-45.

Angel candle holders wearing gold halos. Vcagco Ceramics. Made in Japan. 4.5" tall. $40-50 pair.

Santa Elf holding white teddy bear. Holly around his head is made of spaghetti art. "Bone China." Napco Ware. Made in Japan. 2" tall. $25-35.

Candle holders with spaghetti art around the hem of dress and face. Commodore. Made in Japan. 4.25" tall. $35-45 each.

Christmas shopper planter. The planter is dark green. The puppy white. Napco Ceramics. Made in Japan #AX2757A. 4.5" tall. $45-55.

Christmas caroler wearing a green dress. Her coat is white with gold splatters. The lantern is black. Napco. Made in Japan #AX2750A. 5" tall. $35-45.

This candy dish is made of fine china. Spaghetti art appears only on the caroler. Napco China Company. Made in Japan. 4.5" tall. $45-55.

Caroler's dress is trimmed in spaghetti art. Her braids are tied with green holly and berries. Her hair is golden. Napco. Made in Japan #625. 5" tall. $35-45.

Christmas shopper with multi-colored package. Napco Ceramics. Made in Japan. 4.75" tall. $35-45.

Christmas bell. Spaghetti art trims her cape. Her wings can't be seen in photo. They are gold. Lefton Exclusives. Made in Japan. 4.5" tall. $40-50.

Angel planter holding muff. Holt Howard.
Made in Japan 1958. 4.5" tall. $45-55.

This pretty Christmas Caroler is carrying a
candy cane and singing a carol. Tilso. Made
in Japan. 5" tall. $35-45.

Christmas shopper with white poodle wearing green bow. She has
blond hair, red gloves, and a red bow on her bonnet. Napco Ceramics.
Made in Japan. 7.5" x 4.75". $45-55.

Angel planter. Nice piece, very pretty.
Colors have not faded. Holt Howard. Made
in Japan 1958. 4.5" tall. $45-55.

This angel has a message under her right arm: "Merry Christmas." Her wings and package are trimmed in gold. The wreath is green. Napco Ceramics. Made in Japan #ILX1700W. 4.75" tall. $30-40.

Christmas Angel dinner bell. Skirt is a pale green like the other angels of this series. Lefton Exclusives. Made in Japan. 4.5" tall. $35-45.

White Santa planter with gold belt. National Potteries Company. Cleveland, Ohio. Made in Japan. 4.75" x 3.5". $45-55.

Christmas shopper. Nice face colors. Like new trim on dress. Excellent piece. Napco. National Potteries Company. Cleveland, Ohio. Made in Japan #SI6972. Sold new for $1.49. 6" tall. $65-85.

Santa's reindeer. Very beautiful and rare. Napco Ceramics. Made in Japan. 5" x 4" long. $60-70 pair.

Santa sleigh planter. Spaghetti art on sleigh only. Green holly with red berries trimmed in gold. Napco. Made in Japan. 4" tall. $45-55.

White Santa planter holding holly leaves and wearing white belt. "Merry Christmas and Good Wishes" written on back. Napco. Made in Japan. 6.5" tall. $45-55.

Santa planter. He's winking with his right eye. Trimmed in gold. This piece is in good shape. Lefton Exclusives. Made in Japan. 5" tall. $40-50.

Christmas angel holds a candle with a halo around its tip. Lefton Exclusives. Made in Japan. 4.5" tall. $40-50.

Fat red Santa with spaghetti art trim. Napco. Made in Japan. 5" tall. $30-40.

Salt and pepper Santa Claus set. Mrs.Claus has a bag full of toys. Napco. Made in Japan. 3.5" tall. $45-55 set.

This Santa is flaked in gold. His legs are plated in gold. His eyes are blue, cheeks pink. He is a shelf sitter. Made to hang something off his foot or to set on the fireplace mantel. Napco. Made in Japan. 4" tall. $40-50.

Pink Christmas poodle wearing gold bells, red bow, and cap. Napco Creations. Made in Japan. 4" tall. $45-55.

Mr. and Mrs. Claus salt and peppers. Mrs. Claus has bag of gifts with candy cane. Napco. Made in Japan. 3.25" tall. $45-55 set.

This Santa is a toothpick holder. Napco. Made in Japan. 6.5" tall. $45-55.

This Santa is a Salt Shaker, dated 1956. Kreiss and Company. Made in Japan. 3.5" tall. $35-45.

105

Two red and white Santas with blue eyes. Napco. Made in Japan. 2.5" tall. $45-55 set.

Santa has open bag on his back to hold candy canes. Napco. Made in Japan. 6.5" tall. $35-45.

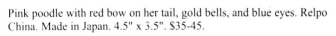

Salt and pepper shakers. All shakers are trimmed in gold. Napco. Made in Japan. Mrs, 3.5" tall; Mr: 3.25" tall. $20-30 each.

Pink poodle with red bow on her tail, gold bells, and blue eyes. Relpo China. Made in Japan. 4.5" x 3.5". $35-45.

Mrs. Santa was not as popular as Mr. Santa. Spaghetti art trims her apron and dress. Napco. Made in Japan #S937F. 6" tall. $35-45.

White Mr. Santa Claus. Napco Ceramics. Made in Japan. 6.5" tall. $40-50.

Salt and pepper set. Basic Christmas colors. Left, 3.5" tall; right, .75" tall. Napco. Made in Japan. $45-55 set.

This Santa Claus is different than most. The star design is a very unusual marking. Napco. Made in Japan. 4" tall. $40-50.

Red and white candle holders. Holt Howard. Made in Japan 1958. 3.5" round. $10-15 each.

Lady angel planter with lots of color. Napco. Made in Japan #AX1699. National Pottery Company. 7.5" tall. $35-45.

Santa candy holder with gold highlights. Spaghetti art shows well. His bag is stamped "Good Wishes." Napco. Made in Japan. $45-55.

Mrs.Claus salt shaker. Inarco. Made in Japan. 3.75" tall. $15-25.

Red Santa. Spaghetti trim is tipped in gold to match belt. Shelf sitting Santa. Eyes are blue and white. Napco. Made in Japan. 4.5" tall. $40-50.

Pretty October angel holds a pumpkin. Vcagco Ceramics. Made in Japan. 5.25" tall. $25-35.

Valentine planter. Spaghetti art around hemline. Girl is holding a bouquet of multi-colored flowers. Gold accents. "Reliable Glassware and Pottery Company." Designed in Hollywood by Reubens. Made in Japan 1956 #A651. 6" tall. $25-35.

Geisha girl. Her kimono has pink and blue flowers. The trim is in gold. Her hair is long strands of spaghetti art. The puppy is short stranded. May be part of a set. Made in Japan. 8" tall. $50-65.

Miscellaneous

Little boy skier with red skis, yellow vest, and spaghetti art on his head. Shafford #2266. Made in Japan. 4.5" x 2.5". $35-45.

White and gold candle holders. Holt Howard. Made in Japan 1958. 3.5" across. $20-30 set.

Long and short strands of spaghetti art with rose accents make up hair and trim on dress. This piece is titled "Betty-Coed." Lefton. Made in Japan. 3.75" tall. $25-45.

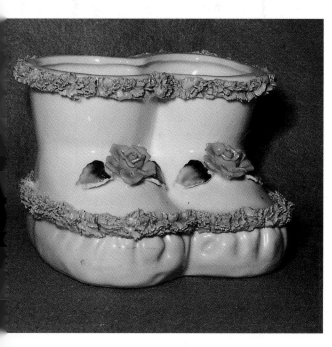

Bootie planter is decorated with pink flowers and blue trim. Reliable Glassware. Made in Japan 1956. $15-20.

This angel's hair and dress are made of long and short spaghetti art. This piece is titled " Little Artist." Lefton. Made in Japan #808B. 3.75" tall. $25-45.

Child planter wearing bunny costume. The face of the child is fine lined and very life like. The bow is blue, ears pink, and the carrot is orange. Napco. Made in Japan #5134A. 5.5" x 3.75". $15-23.

Little Red Riding Hood planter with basket full of pink roses. Spaghetti art very full and well defined. Relpo Original Ceramics. Chicago, Illinois. Made in Japan. 6.5" x 4.75". $45-55.

The girl is wearing white dress with pink rose accents on the bodice and a pink fabric glued on for her bloomers. Her pups have a single pink rose on top of their heads. All three pieces are trimmed and have gold accents. Eyes are blue, white, and black. Lefton. Made in Japan. 4.5" tall. $40-50 set.